W.C

D0182789

French for Catering Students

JUNE 4TH.
FRENCH EXAM (P 108.)

French for Catering Students

John Grisbrooke

BA (Hons) Dip Sorbonne FIL ACP Cert Ed
Senior Lecturer in Modern Languages
Ware College
Hertfordshire

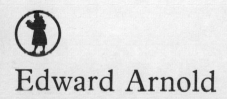

Edward Arnold

© John Grisbrooke 1982

First published 1982
by Edward Arnold (Publishers) Ltd
41 Bedford Square London WC1B 3DQ

Edward Arnold (Australia) Pty Ltd, 80 Waverley Road, Caulfield East,
Victoria 3145, Australia

Reprinted 1984

British Library Cataloguing in Publication Data

Grisbrooke, John
    French for catering students.
    1. French language   2. Cookery—Terminology
    I. Title
    448′.0024642   TX349

    ISBN 0-7131-0710-3

Text set in Compugraphic 10/11pt Plantin
by Colset Private Limited
Printed and bound in Great Britain by Richard Clay
Bungay, Suffolk

Contents

Foreword

The aim of this book is to introduce culinary French to students entering the catering industry. With the needs of students very much in mind, its approach has been geared to courses such as those leading to the City and Guilds 705 and 706 series examinations but it will also prove useful to students taking a French module in TEC catering courses (the former OND/C examinations) and will provide ample revision for those on higher level courses in the hotel and catering industry.

Although the book has primarily been produced for teaching purposes, it can be used as a reference book for checking the accuracy of menu French but it cannot be considered exhaustive in this respect as it is above all an introduction to the subject.

The book contains 27 teaching units with accompanying exercises for use in the classroom or as homework and some additional assignments for preparation out of class. There are five phased revision tests and five aural comprehension exercises as well as three general test papers at the end of the book covering all the work taught in the culinary section.

The language content has deliberately been limited to those aspects of French grammar which are needed for drawing up correctly written menus in French or for conversations involving ordering meals. The main teaching principle of the book is that of association of terms which is reinforced through the type of exercise provided. It is assumed that the usual aspects of language learning (spelling, pronunciation, comprehension) which require so much attention will be dealt with by the teacher during the normal course of lessons.

Catering students are generally very interested in recipes and methods of preparation. While the main aim of the book is to teach French, the student's general and professional education can be enhanced by the use of out-of-class assignments on differences of preparation or dedication. Some guidance as to the type of assignment that can be set is given in the early units, but the timing and choice of such assignments is best left to the discretion of the tutor in the light of the interests of the class. By way of further example, it would be appropriate as an out-of-class assignment to ask students for the recipe for 'sabayon' or 'sauce Réforme' or for the origins of the dedications 'Parmentier' or 'Clamart.'

The choice of what to include or omit in an introductory work is somewhat arbitary and students should be encouraged to enlarge the basic content for themselves as they meet new expressions during their course of study. This will particularly apply to the units of the preparation of meat dishes and sauces. It is also possible to some extent to vary the order in which the various items are taught because of the unit form in which the book has been compiled. Certain units could be omitted to meet the contingencies of a college course while the section on French wines can be taught separately and the three associated multiple choice exercises can be used as test papers or research questions. It is intended that this flexible approach will be beneficial to catering students and helpful to college tutors in the planning of their culinary French courses.

Acknowledgements

I should like to place on record words of appreciation for the helpful advice, suggestions and guidance I have received from many sources. In particular I should like to express thanks to my wife for her constant encouragement and unerring professional judgement, to M E Allison of Westminster College for such excellent technical and linguistic advice, to my colleague, Joëlle Roberts, for her close scrutiny of the text and perceptive observations on the content and not least to Hilary Oughton of Ware College for so painstakingly typing a very tricky manuscript.

I should also like to refer to the use I made of Dr. David Atkinson's 'Menu French', especially in the matter of capitalization.

JG

Unit 1

Menu format

Aim: To teach the different types of menu and associated French terms

Section A Types of menu

Although there are various types of menu, all of them have the same basic pattern or format. You must learn to recognize the different types of menu and, at the same time, learn to distinguish between variations in use and layout because these will vary according to the circumstances in which the menu is presented.

The four basic types of menu are:

1 table d'hôte,
2 prix fixe,
3 à la carte,
4 formal, banqueting, reception or party menu.

1 The 'table d'hôte' menu is very similar to the 'prix fixe' menu, the latter being the term in general use in France. It is a menu with a set number of courses, usually three or four, with a limited choice at each course and offered at a given price. A choice may be given within any of the courses possibly involving a supplementary payment. Coffee may also be included but rarely any alcohol.
2 'Prix fixe' is a term widely used in France to indicate a set menu with little or no choice in any section, offered at a set price. Taxes and/or the cover charge can sometimes be included in the 'prix fixe' menu, for which the term 'tout compris' or 'taxe et service compris' is used.

The opposite of this term is 'non compris',

eg service non compris,
taxe et service non compris.

A drink, generally wine or beer, may also be included in the 'prix fixe' menu. These expressions are met like this:

Menu à x francs tout compris
Menu à x francs taxe et service compris
Menu à x francs service non compris
Menu à x francs service en plus (or en sus) vin en plus (en sus)

The terms 'en plus' and 'en sus' are both used to indicate an additional payment; the former expression is much more common.

1

The service charge is usually calculated at 10–15% of the total price of the bill. Obviously a menu with 'service non compris' or 'service en plus (sus)' will have the service charge added to the total cost of the meal.

3 An 'à la carte' menu has all the dishes individually priced and the customer chooses the meal from the dishes offered. It is usually a more expensive way of eating because of the element of choice which is involved. However, it has great attraction for the customer in that a selection can be made according to individual taste and appetite. In the case of an 'à la carte' meal, it is very unusual for the service or tax to be included (compris) and the customer may also be asked to pay a cover charge (couvert).

A cover charge may be applied to any menu but it is less common for set menus. It is usually levied to meet the costs of place settings, linen or special equipment used in the service.

4 Special menus are drawn up for dinners, receptions, banquets, parties, generally at the request of an organization and in consultation with it. Good examples of this type of menu would be a firm's annual dinner, a wedding reception, a birthday party or much more formally, a diplomatic reception. Very often wine or drinks, coffee and maybe liqueurs are included in the agreed price. There is rarely any variation at any course, since the menu as a whole is agreed, costed and priced before the function.

Section B Layout of the menu

A menu is made up of several sections or 'courses' and there is an accepted order in which they are served. This order of service is given below but it would be very unusual for all these courses to appear on any one menu, although a full 'à la carte' menu could well include all the sections. A 'table d'hôte' menu would include perhaps five to eight courses.

The accepted order of service is:

Course	English	French
First	'starter' (hors-d'oeuvre)	hors-d'oeuvre
Second	soups	potages
Third	farinaceous dishes	(pâtes)
Fourth	egg dishes	oeufs
Fifth	fish	poissons
Sixth	'entrée'	entrées
Seventh	roast	rôtis
Eighth	grills	grillades
Ninth	cold buffet	buffet froid
Tenth	vegetables	légumes
Eleventh	sweets	desserts/entremets
Twelfth	savouries	–
Thirteenth	cheese	fromages*
Fourteenth	fruits	fruits

Coffee, petits fours, liqueurs are served at the end of the meal.

* It is interesting to note that if both cheese and dessert are served, the cheese is served after the dessert in the United Kingdom, whereas it is French practice to serve cheese before the dessert.

Here are some examples of different types of menu.

It is not normal practice to give the various names of each course on a table d'hôte or 'prix fixe' menu, although a clear distinction between each course must be shown. On an 'à la carte' menu various headings may be included.

1 *Prix fixe (Evening meal), four courses, very simple*
    Potage
    ———

    Rôti de boeuf
    ———

    Pommes frites
    ———

    Fruits
    ———

2 *Table d'hôte (Lunch-time) six courses*
    Hors-d'oeuvre variés
    ———

    Oeufs durs mayonnaise
    ———

    Filets de sole bonne-femme
    ———

    Escalope de veau   *veal*
    Selle d'agneau   *lamb .*
    ———

    Petits pois
    Pommes frites
    ———

    Fromage ou Fruits

3 *A la carte*
    Service et boisson en plus

Hors-d'oeuvre	Pommes à l'huile
	Oeufs durs mayonnaise
	Salade russe
	Pâté maison
Potages	Crème St-Germain
	Crème d'asperges
	Potage julienne
Oeufs	Oeufs farcis
	Omelette nature
	Omelette au jambon
Poissons	Colin froid à la mayonnaise

3

	Saumon froid à la mayonnaise
	Filet de sole Véronique
Entrées	Rognons sautés sauce madère
	Foie d'agneau
	Saucisses de Francfort
Rôtis	Poulet rôti
	Gigot d'agneau
Grillades	Côtelette de porc
	Entrecôte grillée
Buffet froid	Assiette anglaise*
	Jambon de Paris*
Légumes	Pommes frites
	Petits pois
	Salade verte
Fromages	Brie
	Camembert
	Roquefort
Desserts	Pâtisserie
	Crème caramel
	Glace
Fruits	Orange
	Pomme
	Banane

* These could appear at the hors-d'oeuvre stage.

Other terms which may appear on the menu to replace the main dish are:

Conseil du chef,
Plat du jour,
Plat recommandé.

One final word about the format of the menu. The 'relevé' which is served between the entrée and the roast has been omitted on the grounds that it is now almost obsolete. In practice the entrée, relevé, rôti and buffet froid have been combined to form the main course, after the fish course and before the vegetable course.

Exercises 1

1 Practise reading all the French terms used in this Unit.
2 What do the following terms mean?
   tout compris   en plus   couvert   service non compris
   prix fixe   boissons
3 Distinguish between à la carte and table d'hôte.
   Why is a menu for a reception unlikely to be 'à la carte'?
   Discuss the advantages for a small restaurant of 'table d'hôte' menus.
4 Explain these terms.
   potage   entrée   buffet froid   fromages   hors-d'oeuvre

4

Put these courses into their accepted order of service.
5 In which section of the menu would you expect to find?
petits pois   saumon   camembert   salade verte
rôti de boeuf   orange   pommes sautées   filet de sole
gigot d'agneau   côtelette de porc
Make sure you know the English equivalent.
6 Using the dishes given in this Unit, make up a five-course meal, lunch or dinner.
7 Go through this Unit making a list of those French terms which are used in English as a matter of course, eg restaurant.

Unit 2

Hors-d'oeuvre 1

Aim: **To teach the French used in fruit- and vegetable-based hors-d'oeuvre**
To introduce the gender of words

Hors-d'oeuvre fall into three main categories:

1 Vegetable- and fruit-based,
2 Meat-, fish- and egg-based,
3 Miscellaneous hors-d'oeuvre.

They can be served as separate dishes or in various combinations, when they form a fairly substantial introduction to a meal known as hors-d'oeuvre variés.
This Unit deals with vegetable- and fruit-based hors-d'oeuvre.

Section A   Salads

Individual vegetables, carefully prepared and attractively decorated and served, form the basis of the 'salade'. Among the most usual examples are:

salade de tomates,
salade de betteraves,
salade de concombre,
salade de chou-fleur,
salade de céleri râpé,
salade de pommes de terre,
carottes râpées,
céleri rémoulade.

With the exception of céleri rémoulade all of these are served with the dressing
  sauce vinaigrette.
A full description would therefore be
  salade de tomates sauce vinaigrette.
Sauce vinaigrette is composed of:
  huile,
  vinaigre (vinaigre de vin, in particular),
  sel,
  poivre,
and then according to taste:
  moutarde,
  ail.
Other dressings possible with certain 'salades' are:

  carottes râpées au jus de citron,
  salade de pommes de terre sauce mayonnaise,
  céleri rémoulade.

It will be seen that the term 'salade' differs very markedly from the English salad.

Section B   Vegetable-based hors-d'oeuvre

The following may also be served individually or as part of an 'hors-d'oeuvre variés'.

  artichauts à la grecque
  fonds d'artichauts *HEARTS*
  asperges à l'huile *OIL*
  avocat (sauce vinaigrette)
  avocat farci *STUFFED*
  olives noires *BLACK*
  olives vertes *GREEN*
  olives farcies
  pommes à l'huile *OIL*
  radis au beurre *BUTTER*
  salade russe
  salade niçoise
  crudités de saison are also served as an hors-d'oeuvre
  RAW VEG

Section C   Fruit-based hors-d'oeuvre

It should be noted that the 'jus' are not a normal feature of French cuisine, served as an hors-d'oeuvre.

  melon   jus de fruits rafraîchis
  melon au porto   jus d'orange
  melon glacé *CHILLED*   jus d'ananas *PINEAPPLE*

melon rafraîchi *CHILLED*   jus de pamplemousse

GRAPE FRUIT. pamplemousse grillé   jus de tomate

pamplemousse rafraîchi

coupe Florida

Language notes

Gender

It is very important to know that all French nouns have gender, either masculine or feminine. Gender is fairly easily recognized because words which are masculine show their gender by having the word 'le', meaning 'the', in front of them:

eg le beurre,
    le sel.

We say therefore that 'beurre' and 'sel' are masculine words.
    Feminine words take the word 'la', also meaning 'the'.

eg la tomate
    la pomme

These two words are then feminine.
    Words beginning with a vowel or a silent 'h' drop the 'e' or the 'a' of 'le' and 'la'. Examples of this are:

l'ail (m),
l'huile (f),
l'olive (f),

In this case to help learn the gender of the word, a small (m) or (f) is put after the word, either in the Unit or in the vocabulary, when the word is first introduced.
    Although it is easy to recognize the gender of a word, gender can be difficult to learn and recall but it must be borne in mind when compiling menus or referring to dishes to ensure accurate French. It is therefore very sound practice to learn the gender of each new word as it is met and to revise genders regularly.

Vocabulary

These are the new words introduced in Unit 2. Their gender is given. The words given in Unit 1 will be reintroduced at a later stage in the book when the genders will be indicated.

Masculine		*Feminine*	
l'ail	garlic	l'asperge	asparagus
l'ananas	pineapple	la betterave	beetroot
l'artichaut	artichoke	la carotte	carrot
le beurre	butter	l'huile	oil

7

Masculine		Feminine	
le céleri	celery	la mayonnaise	'mayonnaise' sauce
le chou-fleur	cauliflower	la moutarde	mustard
le citron	lemon	l'olive	olive
le concombre	cucumber	la pomme de terre	potato
le jus	juice	l'orange	orange
le melon	melon	la rémoulade	'rémoulade' sauce
le pamplemousse	grapefruit	la salade	salad
le poivre	pepper	la sauce	sauce (gravy)
le radis	radish	la tomate	tomato
le sel	salt	la vinaigrette	'vinaigrette' sauce
le vinaigre	vinegar		

Exercise 2

1 What methods of preparation have so far been given for
   tomate   pamplemousse   melon?
2 Complete the following terms:
   salade de céleri ———— pommes ———— carottes ————
   jus de ———— radis ———— artichauts à la ————
   What gender are all the words in the exercise?
3 Basing your answers on Unit 2 only, what can be served:
   sauce vinaigrette   à l'huile   rafraîchi   vertes   mayonnaise?
4 Give the ingredients (in French with their gender) of sauce vinaigrette
   with the variants.

Preparation

1 What fruits are used in 'coupe Florida'? Check in a cookery book.
   Give the fruits in French with their gender.
2 Which vegetables would you expect to find in 'crudités'?
3 What are the ingredients in a 'salade niçoise' and a 'salade russe'?
   Give the ingredients in French with their gender.
4 What ingredients do you need for sauce rémoulade?

Unit 3

Hors-d'oeuvre 2

Aim: To teach the French for hors-d'oeuvre based on meat, fish and eggs
To introduce plurals of nouns
To introduce the use of 'à la'

This is the second unit devoted to hors-d'oeuvre. This time all the hors-d'oeuvre introduced are meat, fish or egg based. A few miscellaneous dishes are added at the end.

Section A   Meat-based hors-d'oeuvre

andouille de Vire *cn·ɒɒɕɪɴ'ɕ SAHSAGE*
assiette anglaise
charcuterie *meat-from pig .*
jambon *HAM*
jambon (cru *RAW*)
jambon (fumé *SMOKED*)
jambon de Bayonne*
jambon de Paris*   *TYPES*
jambon au (beurre *BUTTER*)
jambon aux (cornichons *GURKINS*
pâté
pâté de (foie *LIVER*)
pâté de foie gras (d'oie)
pâté (maison *MADE BY CHEF*)
pâté de (campagne *COUNTRY*)
pâté en croûte *IN A CRUST*
(POUNDED) rillettes de porc
MEAT rillettes de Tours*
PORK rillettes du Mans*
salami
saucisson sec (au beurre)
saucisson à l'ail
saucisson au (poivre *PEPPER*)
terrine *POTTED MEAT ·*

* Just as certain British dishes have the qualification of a town or region, eg Norfolk turkey, Aylesbury duckling, so French dishes may have this description. It will indicate a difference in method of preparation.

Section B Fish-based hors-d'oeuvre

anchois aux oeufs durs
   filets d'anchois
bouquets mayonnaise
caviar
crevettes roses
fruits de mer SEA] shell fish
harengs à la portugaise TOMATO SAUCE.
huîtres   (la douzaine
          la demi-douzaine)
sardines à l'huile OIL
saumon fumé SMOKED.
thon à l'huile TUNA
truite fumée TROUT SMOKED.

Section C Egg-based hors-d'oeuvre

oeufs durs mayonnaise*
oeufs mayonnaise*
oeufs farcis
* Both terms are met.

Section D Miscellaneous

andouillettes
escargots de Bourgogne (la douzaine)*
* These can also appear at the fish course.

Language notes

Plurals

Many words appear on the menu or are used in ordering in the plural form.
The plural of 'le', 'la' or 'l'' is 'les'.

eg le melon les melons
    la tomate les tomates
    l'olive les olives

It must be noted that the word itself adds an 's'
   sardines, crevettes, oeufs.
If the word already ends in 's' in the singular, it does not change:
   l'anchois les anchois.
There is also a question of pronunciation to consider. If the word begins
with a vowel or silent 'h', the 's' of 'les' elides with the following word:
   les olives   les anchois   les escargots   les huîtres

10

The term 'à la'

The term 'à la' or 'à l' before a vowel or a silent 'h' has been used several times already. It has two meanings which must be clearly differentiated.

The first meaning is 'in the style of'. In this case it stands for a shortened form of the expression 'à la mode'

eg à la portugaise = à la mode portugaise
    à la grecque   = à la mode grecque

Its second meaning is 'garnished with'. Examples of this are:

à l'ail,
à l'huile.

It is important to understand that 'à la' becomes 'au' when it is used with a masculine noun. Hence the importance of gender mentioned in Unit 2. Examples so far met are:

au beurre,
au poivre.

Both 'au' and 'à la' become 'aux' when standing before plural nouns. Examples of this are:

aux cornichons,
aux anchois.

Exercise 3

1 Complete the following basing your answers on Unit 3.
———— de Bayonne ———— fumé ———— maison
———— mayonnaise ———— la douzaine.
2 Explain the significance of the following descriptions:
jambon *de Paris* pâté *maison* saucisson *à l'ail*
harengs *à la portugaise* huîtres (*la douzaine*)
3 Give the gender of these words.
jambon saumon pâté caviar terrine ocuf
Which items above would these terms accompany?
de foie gras farci fumé cru
4 Write and say the following words in the plural:
la sardine l'anchois l'oeuf le cornichon la crevette
5 From Unit 2 find a vegetable-based hors-d'oeuvre using 'à la' with the meaning of:
in the style of,
garnished with.

Vocabulary

Masculine		*Feminine*	
l'anchois	anchovy	l'andouille	'andouille' sausage
le bouquet	prawn	l'assiette	plate
le caviar	caviare	la campagne	country
le cornichon	gherkin	la charcuterie	pork butcher's meat
le filet	fillet	la crevette	shrimp
le foie	liver	la douzaine	dozen
le fruit	fruit	l'oie	goose
le hareng	herring	la croûte	crust, pastry
le jambon	ham	la sardine	sardine
l'oeuf	egg	la terrine	terrine; 'terrine' dish
le pâté	pâté		
le porc	pork		
le salami	salami sausage		
le saumon	salmon		
le thon	tuna; tunny		

Words in the plural

les crevettes (f)	shrimps	les huîtres (f)	oysters
les escargots (m)	snails	les rillettes (f)	'rillettes'

Unit 4

Soups (les potages)

Aim: To teach French terms associated with soups
To introduce descriptive terms and dedications

Soups are classified as clear or thick soups. The general term for a clear soup is 'consommé'. According to the method of preparation, thickened soups are:

> purée,
> crème,
> velouté.

'Potage' is the most general term used for soups, particularly of a vegetable origin. It is used frequently in the term 'potage du jour'.

'Soupe' is used exclusively in the naming of certain individual soups.

'Bisque' is a soup made with a basis of shellfish.

Section A   Consommés

Beef consommé is by far the most widely served. Here are the more usual examples:

consommé de boeuf,
consommé froid en gelée, *gelled consomme.*
consommé de gibier, *game*
consommé de poisson, *fish*
consommé de volaille. *chicken.*

'Consommés' can be flavoured 'au fumet de ......',

consommé au fumet de céleri,   *essence of celery*
consommé au fumet de tomate.   *tomatoe*

Garnishes are sometimes added and the 'consommé' is then known by the garnish:

consommé brunoise,   *garnish - diced veg*
consommé Crécy,   *carrot*
consommé julienne,   *fine strips of veg*
consommé madrilène.   *celery tomatoes RED PEPPERS.*

Further possible garnishes are 'royales' and these vary according to the flavour imparted to the 'royales':

thin Soup
consommé royale,   *~~poached~~ chicken.*
consommé crème royale,   *cream*
consommé royale St-Germain*,   *peas*
consommé royale Crécy*.   *carrots.*

* See Section C page 14.
Other specialized consommés are

croûte-au-pot,   *~~BEEF BROTH~~ ONIONS*
petite marmite, —   *STOCK POT.*
bouillon.   *STOCK.*

Consommés are often served 'en tasse' ← *IN CUP.*
consommé en tasse.

Section B   Thickened soups

As we have already seen, thick soups vary in name according to their method of preparation. They are:

crème,
purée,
velouté.

a) *Crèmes* Cream soups can be identified firstly by direct reference to the principal flavouring. Examples of this are:

13

crème d'asperges,
crème de céleri,
crème de champignons, *MUSHROOMS*
crème de tomates,
crème de volaille, *POULTRY .*

They are secondly identifiable by a description which indicates the main ingredient.
Examples of this are:

crème Du Barry*, *CAULIFLOUR .*
crème St-Germain*, *Peas .*
crème Parmentier*. *POTATO'S.*

* See Section C below.

These descriptions or culinary terms should be learned as part of French terminology, since they appear at various other points in the course, conveying the same flavour or garnish.

b) *Purées*   Purées are also identified in the same way either by a direct reference to the main ingredient or by use of a descriptive term which implies what that ingredient is.

purée cressonnière *CRESS*
purée de lentilles
purée de pois *Peas.*
purée de légumes *VEG .*
purée St-Germain *Peus .*
purée Parmentier *POTATO'S*

The terms may also appear with the word 'potage'.

potage Crécy *CARROTS.*
potage St-Germain *Peas .*
potage cressonnière *CRESS ;*
potage Parmentier *POTATO'S*

Occasionally the special property of the soup is given as a more general term which can also be applied to other aspects of preparation or service of dishes other than soups. These are the soups:

potage bonne-femme, *MINCED LEAKS POTATO'S*
potage fermière, *FARMERS SOUP VEG .*
potage julienne,
potage garbure (used only with soup).

Velouté means velvety. This term gives an idea of the consistency of a *velouté*

Section C   Descriptive terms

It is always very useful to have a list of descriptive terms readily available.

14

The more common ones are given here and students should be able to associate the term with the principal flavouring.

    Crécy CARROT·
    portugaise TOMATO
    flamande
    florentine SPINACH·
    St-Germain PEAS
    Parmentier POTATOS
    provençale PROVENCE
    lyonnaise ONIONS·
    Du Barry CAULIFLOWER.

As we have seen, they are used in the following way:

    purée Parmentier*,
    crème Du Barry*,
    potage Crécy*.

* Two points must be noted about these descriptive terms.
1 The descriptive term may be a dedication to a person or place,

eg Du Barry   Mme du Barry
    St-Germain the saint
    Crécy   a town in northern France (or possibly a town in the
                département of Seine-et-Marne)

In this case, the descriptive term always has a capital letter.
2 The descriptive term may also be an adjective derived from a country, region or town.

eg portugaise   from Portugal
    provençale from Provence in southern France
    lyonnaise   from Lyon, a city in central France

In these cases, the adjective always has a small first letter.

Section D Types of soup

a) *Soupes* The term 'soupe' is reserved for a small number of soups.
    soupe à l'oignon ONION
    soupe aux rognons KIDNEYS·
    soupe de poissons FISH·
b) *Bisques* The two most well-known bisques are:
    bisque de homard, LOBSTER·
    bisque d'écrevisses. CRAYFISH·
c) Finally there are few soups which have special names.
    potage queue de boeuf lié OXTAIL SOUPE
    potage fausse tortue clair MOCK TURTLE SOUPE
    potage fausse tortue (lié THICKENED)
THICK→velouté) Agnès-Sorel
    vichyssoise → POTATO. LEEK SOUPE·

15

These lists are in no way exhaustive. Students are urged to extend their knowledge of soups and to add others they meet in the course of their work to the basis given here.

Vocabulary

Masculine		Feminine	
bouillon	'bouillon'	bisque	'bisque'
champignon	mushroom	crème	cream
consommé	'consommé'	écrevisse	crayfish
fumet	'fumet'	garbure	'garbure'
gibier	game	gelée	jelly, aspic
homard	lobster	lentille	lentil
jour	day	marmite	stockpot
oignon	onion	purée	purée
pois	pea	queue	tail
poisson	fish	royale	'royale'
pot	pot	soupe	soup
potage	soup	tasse	cup
rognon	kidney	tortue	turtle
velouté	'velouté'	volaille	game birds; poultry

Exercise 4

1 Distinguish between these soups:
consommé   crème   bisque   soupe   velouté
2 What are?
royale   brunoise   potage du jour   madrilène   fumet
3 What flavour or ingredient do you associate with?
Crécy   St-Germain   Parmentier   cressonnière
Du Barry   portugaise
4 In terms of this Unit complete the following:
bisque ——   —— aux rognons   queue de boeuf ——
—— fermière   —— royale St-Germain
5 Give the French for the following soups:
cream of mushroom   cream of chicken   oxtail   carrot   potato
6 What soup would you make with the following as principal ingredients?
watercress   lobster   mixed vegetables   lentils   kidneys

16

Unit 5

Fish and shellfish (poissons et crustacés)

Aim: **To teach the French names of the commoner varieties of fish and seafood**
To introduce the French for cuts of fish

Fish can be classified in the following way:

Round Fish   a) White eg   whiting, haddock,
           b) Oily   eg   herring, trout.
Flat Fish   a) White eg   sole, plaice,
           b) Oily   eg   skate.
Other seafood, 'fruits de mer', are classified as
           a) Crustaceans,
           b) Molluscs.

Section A   French names for fish

These are the French names for the commoner fish, according to the above category.

a) Round White   aiglefin (m)
                  cabillaud (m)
                  colin (m)
                  merlan (m)
                  morue (f)
b) Round Oily   anchois (m)
                  hareng (m)
                  maquereau (m)
                  sardine (f)
                  saumon (m)
                  truite (f)
c) Flat White   flétan (m)
                  plic (f)
                  sole (f)
                  turbot (m)
d) Flat Oily   raie (f)

The principal crustaceans are:

bouquet (m), *PRAWN.*
crabe (m), *CRAB*
crevette (f), *PRAWN*
écrevisse (f), *CRAYFISH*
homard (m), *LOBSTER.*
langouste (f), *SPINY LOBSTER. CRAWL*
langoustine (f). *SCAMPI*

The principal molluscs are:

coques (f), *COCKLES*
huîtres (f), *OYSTERS*
moules (f). *MUSSELS.*
COQUILLE   SCALLOPS.

Section B   Cuts and methods of preparation

These terms are in common usage for cuts of fish:

filet, *FILLET*
délice, *"*
suprême, *STEAK*
darne, *STEAK*
tronçon, *STEAK*
paupiette, *STRIP*
goujon. *STRIP.*

Examples of the use of these terms are:

filet de sole, ⎤
délice de sole, ⎦ *FILLET*
suprême de cabillaud, ⎤ *COD STEAK*
darne de saumon, ⎦ *SALMON STEAK.*
goujon de sole, ⎤ *STRIPS*
paupiettes de sole ⎦

Vocabulary

Masculine		*Feminine*	
aiglefin*	haddock	anguille	eel
cabillaud	cod	coque	cockle
colin	hake	darne	steak, cutlet
coquillage	shellfish	langouste	spiny lobster
crabe	crab	langoustine	small lobster
délice	fillet	moule	mussel
flétan	halibut	morue	cod (dry)
four	oven	paupiette	'paupiette'
goujon	'goujon', strip	plie	plaice
maquereau	mackerel	raie	skate

18

Masculine		Feminine	
merlan	whiting	sole	sole
suprême	fillet		
tronçon	steak (fish)		
turbot	turbot		

* See Glossary for alternative spellings.

Exercise 5

1 Give the general classification of fish and shellfish.
2 State into which category the following fish fall:
  colin   saumon   sardine   raie   cabillaud   homard
  langouste   huître   maquereau   anchois
3 State the gender of the items mentioned in the previous exercise.
4 Which words in exercise 2 are most likely to be used in the plural? Write them in the plural form.
5 Describe the following cuts:
  darne de cabillaud   suprême de cabillaud
  tronçon de saumon   filet de plie   paupiettes de plie
6 Which of the fish mentioned are more likely to be used at the hors-d'oeuvre course?
  By reference to other cookery books and Unit 3, draw up a list of fish-based hors-d'oeuvre.

Unit 6

Fish – methods of preparation and service

Aim: To teach the French for various methods of fish service and preparation with particular reference to agreement of adjectives.

Section A   Agreement of adjectives

Great care must be taken in drawing up the French which is used to describe the methods of service or preparation of fish dishes. Some of the commoner ways of cooking fish are:

    frit, poché, grillé, fumé.

These words are adjectives in this context and adjectives in French must agree with the word they describe. They agree in number and gender with the word they accompany. Number means that the word they accompany is either singular or plural and gender means that the word is either masculine or feminine. In the list above 'poché' is the masculine singular form: it must therefore be used with a masculine singular word,
eg saumon poché.

The feminine singular form is 'pochée', the masculine plural form is 'pochés' and the feminine plural form is 'pochées'.

Put another way, the adjective will vary in spelling and perhaps pronunciation according to the word it accompanies.

Example 1 We will look at the word 'grillé'.

masculine singular	:	hareng grillé
masculine plural	:	filets de sole grillés ('grillés' agrees with 'filets')
feminine singular	:	sole grillée
feminine plural	:	sardines grillées

Example 2 As a further example we will look at the use of the word 'frit'. This too has four spellings depending on the use of the word.

	masculine	feminine
singular	frit	frite
plural	frits	frites

There is in this case a noticeable change in pronunciation.

So to summarize, unless otherwise stated the rule for the agreement of adjectives can be put in this table form:

	masculine	feminine
singular	(−)	−e
plural	−s	−es

Section B   Agreement of adjectives and descriptive terms

Having learned the rule about the agreement of adjectives, we can now see how it applies to various other methods of preparation or serving. These will vary according to the fish introduced in Unit 5.

blanchaille	blanchailles frites
cabillaud	darne de cabillaud grillée
	darne de cabillaud pochée
	suprême de cabillaud frit
hareng	hareng grillé sauce moutarde
merlan	filets de merlan frits
	merlan en colère meunière*
plie	filet de plie frit
	filets de plie grillés
saumon	darne de saumon pochée

	darne de saumon grillée
	suprême de saumon poché
	saumon fumé
	saumon froid sauce mayonnaise
sole	soles grillées
	goujons de sole frits
truite	truites grillées
	truites meunière*
	truites aux amandes
turbot	turbot poché

* It is a little perplexing to notice that in the case above 'truites meunière' the word 'meunière' does not agree. Some words which appear to be adjectives are a shortened form of the 'à la' construction, meaning 'in the manner of'. Meunière is a good example of this. Thus we must write:

filets de sole meunière,
truite meunière,
soles meunière.

Further examples of this practice are:

bonne-femme	sole bonne-femme
Véronique	sole Véronique, filets de sole Véronique
dieppoise	filets de plie dieppoise

In the case of descriptive terms, like meunière, the list is very long and students are advised to add to the list started here from the examples they meet during the course of their training.

There are other methods of preparation which do not use adjectives but descriptive terms. These too should be learned:

en colère	merlan en colère
au gratin	cabillaud au gratin
à l'anglaise	merlan à l'anglaise
au beurre noir	raie au beurre noir
au vin blanc	filets de sole au vin blanc
au bleu	truite au bleu

Fish specialities

Certain quite common fish or shellfish-based dishes do not fall into the categories already studied. These are:

bouillabaisse,
brochet,
quenelles de brochet,
coquillages,
coquille St-Jacques,
fruits de mer,
laitance,

21

moules marinière,
mousse de saumon,
quenelle de crevettes,
soupe de poisson.

The following are fish commonly served in France which are less popular in the United Kingdom:

daurade au four,
lieu,
lotte à l'armoricaine,
rouget.

Vocabulary

Masculine		*Feminine*	
brochet	pike	amande	almond
gratin	'gratin'	blanchaille	whitebait
lieu	pollack	bouillabaisse	'bouillabaisse'
rouget	red mullet	daurade	dorado, sea bream
vin	wine	laitance	roe
		lotte	burbot
		mousse	'mousse'
		quenelle	'quenelle'

Exercise 6

1 Add the word 'poché' in its correct form to the following:
saumon   darne de saumon   cabillaud
suprême de cabillaud   turbot
2 Add the word 'grillé' in its correct form to the following:
sardines   goujons de sole   hareng   saumon   sole
3 Add a word which agrees with the following:
——— pochée   ——— frit   ——— grillées
——— grillé   ——— pochés
4 With which fish do you associate the following method of preparation?
en colère   Véronique   au beurre noir   au bleu   fumé
5 Give a suitable preparation for the following:
filet de plie   turbot   suprême de cabillaud   truite   saumon
6 What are the following?
bouillabaisse   goujons   beurre noir   au bleu   meunière

Further work on adjectives

The following dishes have been taken from the previous Units. Comment on the adjective agreements in each case:

oeufs farcis,
rognons sautés,
pommes frites,
salade verte,
carottes râpées,
céleri braisé,
olives noires,
beurre noir,
melon glacé,
crevettes roses,
fausse tortue liée.

Take each adjective and apply it to another dish. Ensure that you get the agreements correct.

The following preparations of fish dishes were taken from a cookery book. Comment in each case on the descriptive part:

merlan à l'anglaise,
maquereaux dieppoise,
sardines farcies,
saumon en gelée,
filets de sole normande,
filets de sole au gratin,
thon braisé,
morue provençale.

Revision test 1 (Units 2 – 6)

1 Hors-d'oeuvre

Give the English for the following terms. If more appropriate, describe the dish or process.

a) *Meat-based*
   jambon   jambon de Bayonne   pâté de foie   pâté maison
   terrine   assiette anglaise   saucisson à l'ail   [7 marks]
b) *Vegetable*
   salade de betteraves   carottes râpées   huile   vinaigrette
   mayonnaise   artichauts   radis au beurre   [7 marks]
c) *Miscellaneous*
   jus d'orange   sardines à l'huile   thon à l'huile
   saumon fumé   oeufs durs   escargots   [6 marks]

2 Soups

a) Give a brief explanation of:
consommé   purée   fumet   crème   soupe   [5 marks]

b) What is the principal ingredient in the following?
potage Crécy   potage flamande   potage Du Barry
potage Parmentier   potage portugaise   [5 marks]

c) Which soup is the odd one out?
crème d'asperge   soupe à l'oignon   crème de tomates
potage cressonnière   potage aux épinards   [1 mark]

d) Give the English for each soup in c).   [5 marks]

e) What are the following?
potage du jour   purée de pois aux croûtons
bisque de homard   royale   [4 marks]

3 Fish

a) Give the general classification of fish and shellfish.   [6 marks]

b) Give the English for:
merlan   morue   colin   saumon   plie   raie
anchois   [7 marks]

In each case indicate the gender of the French word.   [7 marks]

c) Give three cuts of fish (in French).   [3 marks]

d) What are the following?
homard   huîtres   moules   coquilles St-Jacques
au bleu   Véronique   meunière   [7 marks]

4 Give the French for the following:

potatoes   carrots   celery   cheese   fruit
In each case indicate the gender.   [10 marks]

80 marks

Unit 7

Vegetables (les légumes)

Aim: To teach the names of vegetables in French
To revise descriptive terms
To learn plurals in 's' and 'x'

Section A   Vegetables and methods of preparation

Several vegetables have already been introduced in the Unit on hors-d'oeuvre. The Unit dealing with soups showed that specialist terms, relating to a place, region, or perhaps a person, may also give an indication of the vegetable served with or as a part of any given dish. This Unit gives the more common vegetables and some methods of preparation, as well as revising the specialist terms used to indicate a garnish or vegetable flavour.

It is important to note that the method of preparation may apply either to an hors-d'oeuvre or to a vegetable course. The student should find out which course the suggested method of preparation applies to.

artichauts (m)	artichauts
	fonds d'artichauts
asperges (f)	asperges au beurre
	pointes d'asperges
	asperges milanaise
aubergines (f)	aubergines farcies
carottes (f)	carottes au beurre
	carottes glacées
	carottes Vichy
céleri (m)	céleri braisé
	céleri au jus
champignons (m)	champignons grillés
chou (m)	chou à l'anglaise
	chou nature
	chou de printemps
choucroute (f)	choucroute alsacienne
chou-fleur (m)	chou-fleur à l'anglaise
	chou-fleur au gratin
	chou-fleur sauce Mornay
	chou-fleur nature
	chou-fleur vinaigrette
	chou-fleur milanaise
choux de Bruxelles (m pl)	
concombre (m)	salade de concombre

courgettes (f) — courgettes à l'anglaise
courgettes farcies
courgettes frites
courgettes provençale

endive (f) — endives belges *chicory Belgium*
endives braisées *braised chicory*

épinards (m) — épinards en branches *leaf spinach*
spinach purée d'épinards *Puree spinach*
épinards à la crème *cream added*

fèves (f) — fèves à l'anglaise *Boiled*
Broad Beans fèves nature *naturel*
fèves au beurre *in butter*

flageolets (m) *same* flageolets à la bretonne *Haricots*

haricots (m) — haricots verts
runner beans haricots à l'anglaise
haricots au beurre *butter*
young peas in pod mange-tout *Dwarf bean yellow*

laitue (f) — laitue *lettuce*

maïs (m) — maïs Washington *Sweet corn*

oignon (m) — oignons braisés *braised onions*
oignons sautés *sauté onions*
oignons frits à la française
(oignon clouté) *studded onion*

panais (m) — panais au beurre

petits pois — petits pois à l'anglaise
petits pois bonne-femme *in juice*
petits pois à la française
petits pois au jus ←
(petits pois à la menthe) *in mint*

poireau (m) — poireaux braisés

pommes — (see following Unit)

tomate (f) — tomates farcies *stuffed*
tomates grillées *grilled*
tomates provençale *Baked.*

Section B   Terms

Other terms closely associated with the use of vegetables are:

F macédoine de légumes — *mixed vegetables*
jardinière *carrots turnips cauli coat with Hol*
printanière *spring veg*
Chopped julienne *strips same size. ?*
mushroom Duxelles *turned carrots turnips beans peas*
shallots Réforme *served with lamb chops garnish bread*
in butter

As a general rule, these words are used in the singular.
The following terms indicate that a vegetable is used as a garnish to the

26

main dish or that that vegetable is the principal ingredient or flavouring of the preparation:

bruxelloise	Brussels sprouts
Clamart	Peas
Crécy	Carrots
Du Barry	Cauliflower
flamande	Cabbage plus carrots
florentine	Spinach
Parmentier	Potato
portugaisc	Tomato
St-Germain	Peas

Examples of the use of this terminology are:

poulet sauté Parmentier,
blanquette de veau Vichy,
carré d'agneau Clamart,
filet de boeuf Du Barry.

There are a few specialist vegetable dishes which fall outside the classification given so far:

ratatouille niçoise,
cassoulet toulousain,
choucroute alsacienne.

Vocabulary

Masculine		*Feminine*	
agneau	lamb	aubergine	aubergine
boeuf	beef	blanquette	'blanquette'
carré	best end	branche	leaf (lit. branch)
cassoulet	'cassoulet'	choucroute	sauerkraut
chou	cabbage	courgette	courgette
chou de Bruxelles	Brussels sprout	endive	chicory
épinards	spinach	fève	broad bean
flageolet	'flageolet' bean	laitue	lettuce
haricot	green bean	ratatouille	'ratatouille'
maïs	sweet corn		
mange-tout	type of 'haricot'		
panais	parsnip		
poireau	leek		
poulet	chicken		
veau	veal		

27

Language notes

In Unit 3 it was seen that nouns make their plural in French by adding 's'. In this Unit, two more rules can be seen in operation:

1 If a word already ends in 's' (or x or z), the word keeps the same spelling in the plural.
eg l'anchois
    le maïs
2 If a word ends in 'eau', it makes its plural by adding 'x'.
eg le poireau
    les poireaux

Exercise 7

1 Explain the spelling of the descriptive term in each of the following:
   artichauts à la grecque   asperges milanaise   carottes glacées
   céleri braisé   courgettes frites   courgettes provençale
2 Which vegetable is indicated by the following garnish?
   Clamart   Crécy   florentine   Parmentier   portugaise
3 What do the following terms means?
   à la française   nature   au jus   au gratin   en branches
   Give a vegetable dish that these terms could be used with.
4 With which vegetables do you associate the following?
   Vichy   farcies   pointes   belges   fonds
5 Complete in a suitable way:
   petits pois ——   aubergines ——
   haricots verts ——   chou ——   épinards ——
6 Add the word 'grillé' in its correct form to each of the following:
   tomates   champignons
   Add the word 'braisé' to each of the following:
   oignons   céleri   endives

Aural comprehension 1

Listen carefully to the words read out to you. State which of the terms given, a), b), c) or d), would accompany the vegetable you hear.
Example: pommes   a) vapeur
                   b) bourguignon
                   c) dieppoise
                   d) au vin
The answer would be a) because the other terms do not accompany 'pommes'.

   Now begin:
1a) grillés   2a) Washington
 b) au beurre   b) à l'anglaise
 c) farcies   c) lyonnaise
 d) Vichy   d) à la menthe

3a)	braisés	**4**a)	grillés
b)	sautés	b)	au jus
c)	provençale	c)	frites
d)	à la française	d)	à l'anglaise
5a)	en branches	**6**a)	au beurre
b)	à l'anglaise	b)	à l'anglaise
c)	belges	c)	grillées
d)	provençale	d)	lyonnaise
7a)	Mornay	**8**a)	de légumes
b)	de Bruxelles	b)	braisé
c)	Clamart	c)	à l'anglaise
d)	Parmentier	d)	nature
9a)	grillées	**10**a)	farcies
b)	nature	b)	frits
c)	salade	c)	en branches
d)	à la menthe	d)	salade

As a written exercise, state another dish or vegetable to which the three wrong choices in each group might apply.

eg Boeuf bourguignon
    Sole dieppoise
    Filet de sole au vin blanc

Unit 8

Potatoes (les pommes de terre)

Aim: To teach some main methods of presenting potatoes

Of all the vegetables, there is no doubt that the potato is the most adaptable.

The following list is obviously not a complete résumé of all the methods of preparation possible but it does give the essential methods. Students should make their own additions as they develop their awareness of the numerous other possibilities. Reference to a good recipe book will supply the difference in presentation.

Methods of preparation

The methods of cooking potatoes are:

   boiling or steaming,
   cooking in the oven with or without fat,

shallow frying,
deep frying.

Section A Boiled or steamed potatoes

pommes à l'anglaise *boiled*
pommes nature *'*
pommes à la menthe *— in mint*
pommes persillées *— parsley potatoes*
pommes en robe de chambre ⎤ *jacket potatoes — over*
pommes en robe des champs ⎦ *boiled*
pommes à la crème *— creamed potatoes (mashed)*
pommes purée (à la crème) *mashed potatoes*
pommes vapeur *— steamed*
pommes nouvelles *news*
pommes à la neige *snow potatoes — sieved*
pommes mousseline *— cream added*

Section B Prepared in the oven

pommes Anna *— ring potatoes rumbaba potatoes*
pommes brioche *— milks and eggs added + butter*
pommes duchesse *— piped potato*
pommes au four *done in the oven*
pommes marquise *duchess potatoes + tomato concass*
pommes fondantes *" " stock added*
pommes rôties *roast potatoes*
pommes gratinées *cheese — mornay sauce*
under grill

Section C Deep fried

pommes dauphine *has egg added like croquettes*
(pommes) frites *chips*
pommes gaufrettes *wafer with holes in*
pommes paille *straw potatoes*
pommes chips *crisp*
pommes allumettes *match stick potatoes*
pommes Pont-Neuf *thick sticks of potatoes*
pommes croquettes *mashed and cooked in bread crum*

Section D Shallow fried

pommes sautées
pommes lyonnaise *in onions + stock*
pommes Parmentier *cubed*

Potatoes can also be moulded and filled:

pommes florentine — *stuffed with spinach + cheese sauce* (handwritten)
pommes Soubise — *" " onion + white sauce* (handwritten)

Exercise 8

1 Read through the list of preparations and explain the use of 'à la' where it is used.
2 Study the agreement of adjectives. Account for the variation in spelling.
3 List the various ways in which potatoes can be served mashed and piped.
4 Check on the use of potato at the hors-d'oeuvre stage.

Throughout catering 347/9 (handwritten)

Unit 9

Egg and farinaceous dishes

Aim: **To teach the various preparation for egg dishes in French**
To teach farinaceous dishes in French
To practise conversation appropriate to ordering a meal

Section A Egg dishes

Other than hors-d'oeuvre, egg-based dishes are usually served at the second stage of the meal, substituting for the fish or the farinaceous course (also studied in this Unit). Certain egg dishes can be served as a main course, omelette in its various forms being the best example.

The following are the more usual methods of preparation. Consider at which stage in the meal each preparation might be served.

Oeufs brouillés — *scrambled eggs* (handwritten)
Oeufs brouillés aux champignons *scrambled eggs + mushroom* (handwritten)
Oeufs brouillés portugaise *" tomatoes + onions* (handwritten)
Oeufs brouillés au foie de volaille *" " chickens liver* (handwritten)
Oeufs en cocotte *eggs cooked in earthenware dish* (handwritten)
Oeufs à la coque *eggs in the shell - soft boiled* (handwritten)
Oeufs durs *hard boiled egg* (handwritten)
Oeufs durs mayonnaise *+ hard egg* (handwritten)
Oeufs mimosa *mashed yolk through a sieve* (handwritten)
Oeufs farcis *stuffed eggs* (handwritten)
Oeufs mollets *soft boiled eggs* (handwritten)
Oeufs pochés *poached eggs* (handwritten)
Oeufs frits (à la poêle) *fried eggs* (handwritten)
Oeufs sur le plat *eggs on a plate cooked.* (handwritten)

31

Many of these egg dishes have a garnish and students should draw up a list of these garnishes as they come across them in the course of their studies. Some commoner examples are:

Oeufs à la portugaise, *tomatoes tonions*
Oeufs florentine, *spinach*
Oeufs Bercy, *white wine sauce*
Oeufs Clamart. *peas*

Omelettes provide a wealth of variation and again it is only possible to mention the more common fillings.

omelette nature *nature*
omelette au fromage *cheese*
omelette au jambon *ham*
omelette Parmentier *potato diced*
omelette espagnole *spanish - onions tomatoes potatoes*
omelette aux champignons *mushrooms*
omelette aux fines herbes *herbs parsley chervil chives,*
omelette portugaise (aux tomates) *tomatoes onions*
omelette mousseline *— ½ whipped cream + egg whites*

Section B Farinaceous dishes

Farinaceous dishes may firstly be served as a course in their own right, in which case they precede the main course, normally substituting for a fish or egg course. They may also accompany the main course served as a vegetable or the more substantial farinaceous dishes may replace the main course itself. Served as an accompaniment, they clearly replace the potato, although a vegetable may be served as well as the farinaceous dish. As the word implies, farinaceous dishes are made mostly from flour.

There are three main divisions of farinaceous dishes:

a) pasta,
b) gnocchi,
c) rice.

Most pasta dishes are of Italian origin and are consequently known by their Italian names. The French for pasta is 'pâtes'.

a) Pâtes
    pâtes au beurre *WITH BUTTER*
    pâtes au gratin *" CHEESE*
    nouilles au gratin *NOODLES "*

Pâtes of Italian origin:

spaghetti bolonaise
spaghetti milanaise *HAM CHEESE TONGE TRUFFLES. MUSH*
spaghetti au gratin *CHEESE*
ravioli *MEAT PACKETS.*
canneloni *TUBES.*

macaroni au gratin
lasagnes

These words of Italian origin are plural. We say 'Je voudrais des spaghetti, des ravioli ...',
vermicelle, ᴛʜɪɴ sᴛʀɪᵖˢ
potage au vermicelle.
Vermicelle is used as a garnish in clear soups.
Pâtes are also available in shapes, such as shells, stars, bows, etc.

b) Gnocchi
     gnocchi à la parisienne
     gnocchi à la romaine
c) Riz Rɪᴄᴇ
     riz ''
     riz pilau, pilaf
     risotto

Vocabulary

Masculine		Feminine	
fromage	cheese	cocotte	'cocotte'
plat	flat; dish	coque	shell
riz	rice	omelette	omelette
		herbe	herb
		pâte	pasta

Exercise 9

1 To which method of preparation of eggs do these terms apply?
   à la coque   aux fines herbes   au jambon   espagnole   frits
   mimosa
2 Give the French for:
   3 methods of cooking eggs by using water,
   3 methods using fat.
3 Which garnish would you expect according to these terms?
   florentine   aux champignons   nature   portugaise   Parmentier
4 At which stage in the meal could the following dishes be served?
   omelette au fromage   oeufs brouillés au foie de volaille
   oeufs durs mayonnaise   oeufs farcis
5 To which of the farinaceous dishes do these terms apply?
   pilaf   bolonaise   au beurre   à la parisienne   au gratin

Conversation one

Au restaurant

```
Menu à ... frs, service compris

      Pâté maison
    Melon rafraîchi
Salade de pommes de terre
       -----

Darne de cabillaud pochée
    Truite au bleu
       -----
```

la serveuse - waitress

Garçon: Bonjour, monsieur.
Client: Monsieur, Bonjour.
Garçon: Que voulez-vous comme hors-d'oeuvre? *what will you have for starter*
Client: Le pâté, s'il vous plaît.
Garçon: Bien, monsieur. Et comme poisson?
Client: Le cabillaud, s'il vous plaît.

1 Practise reading this conversation.
2 Vary the answers the customer gives
  a) by reference to the menu above;
  b) by reference to the chapters on hors-d'oeuvre and fish.
  (Notice that the customer uses *le* pâté and *le* cabillaud. Consider what the answers would be if he ordered 'salade', 'truite'.)
3 Compose other possible conversations based on simple menus compiled from the units studied so far.
4 Practise reading any menus compiled for general aural comprehension.

Preparation

Make a collection of noodle and pasta boxes and wrappers as a group project.

34

Unit 10

Meat 1 (la viande)

Aim: To teach the French for the cuts of meat as appropriate to menus

To teach methods of preparation and in particular those appropriate to beef

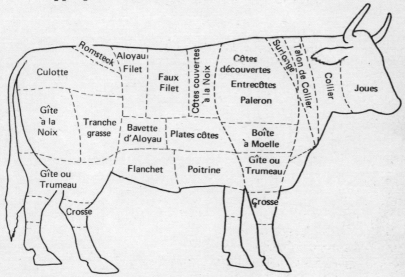

Section A Kinds and cuts of meat

There are four principal sources of butcher's meat:

1 boeuf (m),
2 veau (m),
3 agneau (m) or mouton (m),
4 porc (m).

In the case of pork and lamb or mutton, the cuts of meat (that is the part of the carcass) frequently apply to the dishes prepared and served. As the cuts of meat from the carcass of beef are obviously very much larger, they are only rarely used as menu terms, since the sections of the carcass have to be sub-divided. Veal joints are sometimes served whole and as such may also appear on the menu.

The principal cuts of meat are as follows: they are given in the accompanying sketch.

35

a) *Boeuf*   2   gîte à la noix
4   culotte de boeuf
6   aloyau de boeuf
7 – 10   côte de boeuf
15   filet de boeuf

(The other cuts, which have not been named, are butchery terms. They are unlikely to be used on menus or in table service and so have deliberately been omitted.)

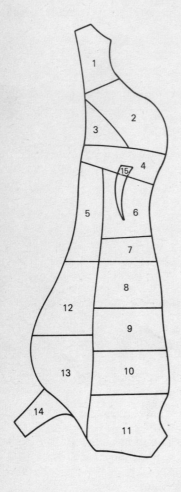

b) *Veau*   cuisseau (m) de veau
longe (f) de veau
carré (m) de veau

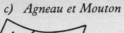

c) Agneau et Mouton   3 carré d'agneau
4 selle (f) d'agneau
5 gigot (m) d'agneau
6 poitrine (f) d'agneau
7 épaule (f) d'agneau
- côtelette d'agneau

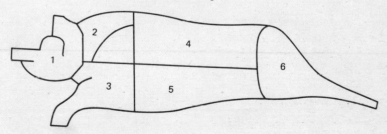

d) Porc   3 épaule de porc
4 longe de porc
5 poitrine de porc
6 cuisseau de porc
- côtelette de porc

Section B   Cuts of meat

Examples of the various cuts of meat used in dishes are given in this section.

a) Boeuf   Noix de boeuf braisée
Aloyau de boeuf rôti
Côte de boeuf rôtie

b) Veau   Cuisseau de veau rôti

c) Agneau   Carré d'agneau persillé
Selle d'agneau rôtie
Gigot d'agneau rôti
Epaule d'agneau farcie

d) Porc   Cuisseau* de porc rôti
* (The spelling cuissot applies to large game only cf Unit 12.)

Section C   Methods of preparation

The principal methods of cooking and preparing meat are:

    rôti   sauté
    braisé   poêlé
    bouilli   pané
    grillé   fricassé *WHITEMEAT*
    farci

As might be expected, the word used as the method of preparation agrees with the cut or meat it describes:

    épaule rôtie,
    boeuf bouilli,
    côtelettes de porc grillées.

Section D   Methods of preparation and serving beef

1 Steaks
  The best-known steaks are:

filet de boeuf	filet de boeuf grillé
entrecôte	entrecôte minute
chateaubriand	
tournedos	tournedos chasseur; tournedos Rossini

Steaks may also be served with a sauce or garnish:
    steak au poivre,
    entrecôte bordelaise.
They are generally grilled in accordance with the wishes of the customer:

    bleu,   *rare*
    saignant, *medium / rare*
    à point,   *medium*
    bien cuit. *welldone*

2 Braising
  There are several well-known dishes where steak is braised.

    carbon(n)ade de boeuf
    contre-filet de boeuf braisé
    boeuf bourguignon (boeuf à la bourguignonne)
    boeuf braisé
    boeuf en daube
    pot-au-feu

3 Assorted preparations

    boeuf braisé à la française
    boeuf braisé à la jardinière
    ragoût de boeuf

paupiettes de boeuf
sauté de boeuf Stroganoff

Vocabulary

Masculine		*Feminine*	
agneau	lamb	carbon(n)ade	carbonade
aloyau	sirloin	côte	rib; side
boeuf	beef	côtelette	chop, cutlet
carré	best end	culotte	rump
cuisseau	leg (veal, pork)	entrecôte	steak
cuissot	haunch	épaule	shoulder
filet	fillet	longe	loin
gigot	leg of lamb	paupiette	'paupiette'
gîte (à la noix)	silverside	poitrine	breast
mouton	mutton; sheep	selle	saddle
porc	pork; pig		
ragoût	stew		
steak	steak		
veau	veal		

Exercise 10

1 To which meat do the following cuts apply?

épaule   cuisseau   gigot   côte   aloyau   carré

2 Match the following pairs:

  a) selle   1 de veau
  b) filet   2 à la noix
  c) poitrine 3 de boeuf
  d) cuisseau 4 d'agneau
  e) gîte   5 de porc

3 Add the word 'rôti' to the following meat or cuts of meat. Make the necessary agreement.

boeuf   selle d'agneau   cuisseau de porc   épaule d'agneau
aloyau de boeuf

4 Complete the following:

——— d'agneau grillées   noix de boeuf ———
poitrine d'agneau ———   ——— bouilli   ——— rôtie

5 Name four steaks, in French.

6 Explain the following terms:

bleu   saignant   tournedos   minute   ragoût

7 What is the principal garnish in these dishes?

steak au poivre   paupiettes de boeuf   carbon(n)ade de boeuf
tournedos Rossini   tournedos chasseur
(Check in a good cookery book.)

8 Explain the following methods of cooking:

fricassé   pané   bouilli   pot-au-feu   poêlé

Unit 11

Meat 2

Aim: **To teach methods of preparation as applied to veal, lamb and pork**
To give further conversation practice in ordering meals

Section A   Veal (veau)

Veal dishes may be prepared

rôti,
braisé,
poêlé, *pot Roast*
pané, *bread crumbs*
sauté, *fried*
fricassé. *stew*

These terms must agree with the cut of meat described:

cuisseau de veau rôti, *leg (m-ls)*
noix de veau braisée, *cushion*
escalope de veau panée, *bread crumbs*
longe de veau rôtie, *loin*
poitrine de veau farcie. *stuffed breast*

Among the principal dishes are:

blanquette de veau, *white stew*
paupiettes de veau, *rolled stuffed fillet of veal*
fricassée de veau, *stew*
rôti de veau, *roast*
sauté de veau Marengo, *butter flour onions white wine tomatoe herbs truffles.*
olive care bread crumbs lemon cinchew escalope de veau viennoise,
escalope de veau milanaise, *tomatoes spaghetti mushroom truffles*
escalope de veau panée,
côtes de veau bonne-femme. *leek potatoe shallots mushrooms*

This list is by no means exhaustive and students should add other preparations, garnishes and methods of cooking as they meet them during the course of their studies.

Section B   Lamb or mutton (agneau ou mouton)

In this section the methods of preparing or serving lamb and mutton have

been extended to show how garnishes may be indicated at the same time.
Among the commoner dishes are:

épaule d'agneau rôtie, *Shoulder*
gigot d'agneau rôti, *leg roast*
carré d'agneau persillé, *best end parsley*
carré d'agneau bonne-femme, *grapes*
longe d'agneau farcie, *stuffed loin*
selle d'agneau niçoise, *saddle tomatoes garlic caper*
côtelettes d'agneau sauce Réforme, *white of egg gherkins mushroom truffels beetroot*
côtelettes d'agneau vert-pré,
côtelettes d'agneau continentale, *continental sauce*
côtelettes d'agneau Henri IV, *Hollandaise chout + tarragon*
filet mignon sauté à la jardinière, *small fillet mixed veg*
filet mignon sauté Clamart, *peas*
noisettes d'agneau à la jardinière, *small mixed veg.*
médaillons d'agneau grillés,
navarin d'agneau aux primeurs, *brown stew onion + potatoes*
ragoût de mouton, *mutton stew*
blanquette d'agneau. *white lamb stew.*

Section C   Pork (porc)

As a main course, pork is mostly served roast or grilled. 'Noisettes' may be served 'sautées'. Examples of the methods of preparation are as follows:

cuisseau de porc rôti,
épaule de porc rôtie,
longe de porc rôtie,
côtelettes de porc grillées,
côtelettes de porc panées.

Section D   Miscellaneous meat dishes

saucisses de porc
saucisses de Francfort à la choucroute
fondue bourguignonne
bouchée à la reine
viande hachée
hachis Parmentier
boudin à l'anglaise

Exercise 11

1 Complete the following:
——— de veau rôtie   escalope de ———
côtelettes de ———   grillées   épaule d'agneau ———
——— de Francfort

2 Explain the following terms:
blanquette   navarin   ragoût   noisettes   hachis
3 With which meat or dish would you associate the following terms?
sauce Réforme   à la reine   Parmentier   viennoise   mignon
4 Put the word in brackets into the correct form of spelling.
gîte à la noix de veau (braisé)   (rôti) de veau   escalope de veau (pané)
côtelettes de porc (grillé)   épaule d'agneau (rôti)
5 By reference to a good cookery book, check on the principal flavouring or
vegetable in the following garnishes:
sauce Réforme   Henri IV   aux primeurs   Clamart   vert-pré

Vocabulary

Masculine		*Feminine*	
boudin	black pudding	blanquette	'blanquette'
hachis	mince	bouchée	large 'vol-au-vent'
médaillon	medal, medallion	escalope	'escalope'
navarin	'navarin'	fondue	'fondue'
primeur	fresh vegetable	noisette	'noisette'

Conversation two

Study this menu.

Salade de tomates

Sardines à l'huile

Pâté maison

Rôti de porc

Blanquette de veau

Navarin d'agneau jardinière

Pommes nature

Pommes frites

Riz

Carottes Vichy

use spring water

Au restaurant

Garçon: Bonjour, monsieur.
Client: Bonjour, Pierre.
Garçon: Que voulez-vous comme hors-d'oeuvre, monsieur?
what do you want as

42

Client:	*lets see* Voyons. La salade de tomates, s'il vous plaît.
Garçon:	Et avec ça? *and with that*
Client:	Le rôti de porc.
Garçon:	Et que prenez-vous comme légumes?
Client:	Je prendrai les frites. *ill have*
Garçon:	C'est tout? *is that all*
Client:	Oui, Pierre, c'est tout.

1 Practise reading this conversation.
2 Read the conversation, changing the customer's replies at each stage.
3 The customer orders: les sardines,
                              la blanquette,
                              les carottes.
  Re-write the conversation, inserting the order at each stage.
4 Using the material you have learned so far, compose other simple menus.
  Read them to the other members of your group for aural comprehension.
5 Practise the term 'Qu'est-ce que vous avez comme .....? '.
  Reply to this question, indicating what choice there is at each stage of the
  menu.

Aural comprehension 2

Listen to the ten sentences read to you. A question will be asked about each
sentence. Answer the questions by choosing a), b), c) or d) according to
which of the suggested answers you think is most suitable.

1 Did the waiter enquire about:
  a) the fish course,
  b) the vegetable required,
  c) the main course,
  d) the hors-d'oeuvre ordered?

2 Did the waiter want to know if
  the customer wanted
  a) the fish course,
  b) a soup,
  c) a vegetable,
  d) chicken?

3 Did the customer order
  a) a side salad,
  b) a vegetable course,
  c) a fish course,
  d) an hors-d'oeuvre?

4 What was the customer's order?
  a) a grilled lamb chop
  b) a grilled pork chop
  c) grilled mushrooms
  d) lamb and grilled
      mushrooms

5 Did the customer order
  a) an hors-d'oeuvre,
  b) a soup,
  c) a main dish,
  d) a vegetable?

6 Did the waiter offer
  a) a fish dish,
  b) a dish with veal,
  c) an hors-d'oeuvre with
      olives,
  d) beef olives?

7 Did the customer order
  a) veal escalope,
  b) a steak,
  c) a pork chop,
  d) sirloin?

8 Did the customer have
  a) chicken and sauté potatoes,
  b) chicken and chips,
  c) steak and game chips,
  d) chicken and match-stick
      potatoes?

9 How did the customer want the steak?
  a) well cooked
  b) rare
  c) medium rare
  d) bloody

10 Which fish dish did the customer have?
  a) grilled salmon
  b) smoked trout
  c) trout with almonds
  d) smoked salmon

Revision test 2 (Units 2 – 11)

1 Methods of preparation and service

Give the English for the following terms:
glacé   au beurre   à l'ail   braisé   persillé   farci
à l'anglaise   frit   au jus   grillé   [10 marks]

2 Fish

a) What are the following fish or crustaceans in English?
  merlan   colin   truite   homard   cabillaud   plie
  hareng   sole   raie   huîtres   [10 marks]
b) In each case give the gender.   [10 marks]
c) Give an appropriate preparation (in French) for the following:
  raie   saumon   truite   sardines   hareng   sole [6 marks]

3 Soups

What is the principal ingredient in:
purée Crécy   purée Du Barry   purée Parmentier
purée flamande   purée portugaise

Give the English for:

crème d'asperges   crème de champignons   purée de pois
bisque de homard   potage aux épinards   [10 marks]

4 Vegetables

Give the English equivalent for:
pointes d'asperges   aubergines   céleri braisé
chou à l'anglaise   chou-fleur au gratin   endives
épinards en branches   panais persillés   poireaux
fèves   [10 marks]

5 Hors-d'oeuvre

Give the English for the following. In some cases, an explanation may be better.

oeufs durs mayonnaise   fonds d'artichauts   thon à l'huile
jus d'orange   olives noires   radis au beurre   escargots
assiette anglaise   charcuterie   jambon cru   [10 marks]

6 Miscellaneous

Complete the following in any appropriate way, other than given in the previous questions.

saucisson ———   carottes ———   jambon ———
pommes ———   pâté ———   ——— farcies   ——— vertes
——— sauce vinaigrette   ——— grillées   ——— à l'anglaise

[10 marks]

7 Match the following pairs:

1 blanquette   a) mollets soft ✓
2 pâtes   b) de porc
3 oeufs   c) pilaf
4 pommes   d) de veau
5 côtelette   e) au beurre
6 gigot   f) d'agneau
7 riz   g) nouvelles NEW ✓

[7 marks]

8 Supply the words which are missing:

jus ... tomate
saumon en gelée
pommes à la crème
pommes au four
consommé de volaille
pommes à l' anglaise
fonds d' artichauts

[7 marks]

90 marks

Unit 12

Offal and game (les abats et le gibier)

Aim: To teach the French appropriate to offal and game

Section A   Offal

Various items of offal are used in the preparation of dishes. These are:

le foie,
le rognon (les rognons),
le coeur,
la langue,
les tripes (f),
les ris (m),
la cervelle.

When served, these should indicate the animal from which they are taken and the method of preparation:

foie d'agneau,
foie de porc,
foie de boeuf.

The principal methods of preparation are:

grillé,
pané,
braisé,
sauté,

so that the full menu term is as indicated:

Foie de veau grillé,
Foie de boeuf braisé,
Foie de veau au lard,
Foie de boeuf lyonnaise.

Other dishes prepared from offal are:

a) *Rognons*   Rognons grillés
Rognons sautés
Rognons sautés Turbigo
Rognons sautés au madère
Rognons à la broche (rognons brochés)

46

b) *Coeur*   Coeur de boeuf braisé   *braised ox heart*
               Coeurs d'agneau braisés   *lambs heart braised*
               Coeurs d'agneau farcis   *stuffed heart*

c) *Langue*   Langue de boeuf sauce madère   *tongue in madeira sauce*
               Langue d'agneau braisée   *tongue of lamb braised (plain)*

d) *Tripes*   Tripes à l'anglaise (lyonnaise)   *type english style onions*
               Tripes à la mode de Caen   *type ox foot onions carrots leeks cloves brandy or rut*

e) *Ris*   Ris de veau à la crème   *creamed sweet breads*
diced bacon   Ris de veau bonne-maman   *sweet bread mushroom onion*
             Ris d'agneau braisés   *lambs tripe braised*

Other dishes derived from edible parts of butcher's meat are:

Queue de boeuf braisée,   *oxtail braised*
Tête de veau en tortue,   *calfs head*
Tête de veau vinaigrette (also an hors-d'oeuvre),   *mushroom quenelle gherkins garlic*
Cervelle au beurre noir.   *fried brains*

entrée   *fried egg*   *vinaigrette scallop veal tongue brain gratons nuggets*

Section B   Game

The term 'gibier' is given to certain wild animals and large birds which are caught and prepared for the table. Included in feathered game are:

le faisan,   *pheasant*
le perdreau (la perdrix),   *partridge (f).*
la caille,   *quelle*
la bécasse,   *woodcock*
le coq de bruyère,   *woodcock*
le grouse,   *grouse*
le canard sauvage.   *duck*   *Should hang for a couple days*

The animals are: (ground or furred game)

le lapin,   *rabbit*
le lièvre,   *hare*
le chevreuil.   *venison.*

Game is very much an acquired taste and features mainly on very specialized menus. Among the more common methods of preparation are:

faisan   faisan rôti   *roast pheasant*
          faisan en casserole   *casserole (BrAISED)*
          faisan en cocotte   *boiled*
roast   faisan poêlé   *post roasted*
bras motions   suprême de faisan   *wing or breast. like fish*
          salmis de faisan   *sauce onion shallots mushroom*
              crouton chervil cook in oil garlic laurel
perdreau   perdreau rôti
roast game - blood   *½ glass red / white*

reduce   *wine brown sauce parsley thyme.*

47

caille   cailles aux raisins   *Quenelle + raison*
          cailles rôties   *" roast*
          cailles en aspic   *un jelly.*

Rabbit in particular and hare to a lesser extent are served more often. The more reputed dishes are:

ragout of fur game

civet de lièvre bourguignonne   *jugged hare stew with*
long hare râble de lièvre   *blood of animal + burgundy*
sauté de lapin   *fried rabbit*
lapin rôti   *roast rabbit.*

cuissot de venaison   *leg of venison*
selle de chevreuil rôtie
civet de chevreuil
hanche de chevreuil
noisettes de chevreuil sautées

Once again it is stressed that the methods introduced here are not the only ways in which game can be prepared. Students should continue to compile their own lists throughout their course.

Vocabulary

Masculine

abats (les)	offal	
canard	duck	
chevreuil	deer; roebuck	
civet	jugged (hare)	
coeur	heart	
coq de bruyère	woodcock	
cuissot	haunch	
faisan	pheasant	
foie	liver	
gibier	game	
lapin	rabbit	
lard	bacon	
lièvre	hare	
perdreau	partridge	
râble	saddle (hare)	
ris	sweetbread	
rognon	kidney	
salmis	stew of game	

Feminine

bécasse	woodcock
broche	spit
caille	quail
cervelle	brains
hanche	haunch
langue	tongue
perdrix	partridge
queue	tail
tête	head
tripe	tripe
venaison	large game

Exercise 12

1 With which item of offal do you associate the following preparations?
Turbigo   à la mode de Caen   au madère   au beurre noir
au lard

48

2 a) Add the word 'braisé' in its correct form to the following:
coeur d'agneau ———— foie de boeuf ————
langue de boeuf ————

    b) Add the word 'sauté' to the following meats, making the agreement:
rognons ———— foie d'agneau ———— cervelle ————

3 Complete with an appropriate method of preparation:
coeur de boeuf ———— tête de veau ————
rognons ———— foie de veau ———— foie de boeuf ————

4 Name in French three examples of feathered game and two examples of furred game.

5 Which game do you associate with the following terms?
———— aux raisins   civet de ————   ———— en cocotte
———— rôti   selle de ————

6 Add the word 'rôti' in its correct form to the following:
hanche de chevreuil   cailles   perdreaux   canard sauvage
bécasses

7 What are?
civet   râble   ris   queue de boeuf   lièvre

Preparation

From a good cook book, check on the method of preparation of
a) salmis,
b) râble.

Unit 13

Poultry (la volaille)

Aim: To teach French terms applied to poultry

'Volaille' is the collective term used for domestic fowl reared for the table. They are occasionally served without being dismembered but it is more usual for them to be served jointed or in portions. The main birds classified as 'volaille', depending on age and size, are:

poulet   chapon   poule   poularde   coq   poussin
canard   caneton
oie   oison
dindon   dinde   dindonneau
pintade   pintadeau

The principal methods of serving are:

rôti,
sauté,
grillé,
poêlé,
braisé,
poché.

Other terms associated with the preparation of fowl are:

fricassé,
suprême de volaille, *best cuts of chicken*
vol-au-vent de volaille,
ballottines. *boned legg stuffed*

While several methods of preparing and serving fowl are traditionally given in English eg Aylesbury duckling, Norfolk turkey, the examples given here are those specifically associated with French.

Poulet poulet rôti
best roas- poulet de Bresse rôti *breast area where chicken*
poulet sauté *fried*
poulet sauté bonne-femme *fried leeks + mushroom*
poulet sauté chasseur *fried in a white wine demiglace*
poulet en cocotte/poulet en casserole
poulet grillé sauce diable *devil sauce*
poulet rôti à l'anglaise *plain roasted*
poulet de grain rôti/grillé *little chicken grilled*
suprême de volaille à la crème *fresh cream*
coq au vin *red wine sauce*
poularde petite mariée
poularde pochée
foies de volailles sautés

This list is by no means complete, since there are numerous methods of preparing chicken. Students should add other methods as they come across them in the course of their training. Familiarity with the whole range of serving chicken is additionally complicated by the garnishes which accompany it. Here are a few examples:

poulet vert-pré
poulet sauté provençale
poulet sauté Parmentier
suprêmes de volaille maréchale

Canard canard à l'orange
canard sauce bigarade
caneton rouennais
caneton braisé aux petits pois
caneton braisé aux navets

50

```
          caneton braisé aux cerises
          caneton poêlé
          canard à l'anglaise
          canard rôti

Oie       oie rôtie à l'anglaise
          oison rôti à l'anglaise
          pâté de foie d'oie (served as an hors-d'oeuvre)

Dindon    dindonneau farci aux marrons
          dindonneau à l'anglaise
          dinde rôtie
```

Many cold dishes are prepared from a basis of 'volaille' to form part of the 'Buffet Froid'. Among the more common dishes are:

```
     mayonnaise de volaille
     pâté de volaille en croûte
     chaud-froid de volaille
     volaille en gelée
     canard en gelée
     mousse de volaille
     mousselines de volaille
     galantine de volaille
     suprêmes de volaille chaud-froid
```

Vocabulary

Masculine		*Feminine*	
canard	duck	ballottine	ballottine
caneton	duckling	casserole	saucepan
chapon	capon	cocotte	stewpan
coq	chicken	croûte	crust
dindon	turkey	dinde	turkey
dindonneau	young turkey	galantine	galantine
navet	turnip	gelée	jelly
oison	gosling	mousse	mousse
pintadeau	guinea fowl (small)	mousseline	muslin; mousseline
poulet	pullet	pintade	guinea fowl
poussin	pullet	poularde	pullet
suprême	suprême	poule	chicken
vol-au-vent	vol-au-vent	oie	goose

Words more commonly found in the plural:

les cerises (f)	cherries
les marrons (m)	chestnut
les petits pois (m)	garden peas

Exercise 13

1 Give five names by which chicken is known.
2 Give the younger equivalent of:
  poulet   canard   oie   dindon
3 Give a definition of the following. Refer to a good cookery book, if in·
  doubt.
  suprême   ballottine   poêlé   chaud-froid   mousseline
4 With what do you associate the following in terms of 'volaille'?
  de grain   en cocotte   chasseur   de Bresse   au vin
5 Complete the following in terms of 'volaille':
  ——— à l'orange   ——— farci aux marrons   ——— maréchale
  pâté de volaille en ———   mayonnaise de ———
6 Complete the following, paying careful attention to agreements:
  ——— rôtie   ——— pochée   ——— sauté   ——— poêlé
  ——— braisé

Unit 14

Cheese (les fromages)

Aim: To teach the names of French (and associated) cheeses
To teach the French for dishes in which cheese is used

The point at which the cheese course is served presents a difficulty for
diners unfamiliar with the French order of service, where the cheese course
has more prominence and precedes the dessert course. There is some logic in
this, in that nowadays, as the cost of wine is high in the United Kingdom, it
would seem preferable to finish any wine with the cheese course. Any wine
taken with the dessert course is usually too sweet to accompany a cheese.
However, it remains a very common British practice to serve cheese as the
last course just prior to coffee.

Section A   Categories

Cheeses introduced in this Unit are predominantly French in origin or those
traditionally associated with French cuisine. Cheeses are categorized as

    hard,
    semi-hard,
    soft or cream cheese.

Where a choice of cheese is offered, one of the following terms is used:

plateau de fromages, *cheese board*
fromages au choix, *choice of cheeses*
fromages assortis. *assorted cheese*

Hard cheese:
The best known hard cheeses are:

gruyère,
emmenthal,
cantal,
comté,
parmesan.

Semi-hard cheese:
Among the better known semi-hard cheeses are:

st-paulin,
port-salut,
pont-l'évêque,
tomme de Savoie.

Soft or cream cheese:
The cream cheeses are:

camembert,
brie,
coulommiers,
carré de l'est,
demi-sel*,
petit suisse*,
fromage frais*.

* May be served with sugar or salt.
Blue:
Among the more prominent blue cheeses are:

roquefort,
bleu de Bresse,
bleu d'Auvergne,
bleu des Causses.

Specialities:

Boursin *goat cheese.*
fromage de chèvre *gold cheese - corsica southd france* *Popular.*

Yoghurt may also be served as a cheese. The French is:

yaourt,
yaourt nature,
yaourt parfumé.

The choice of flavours is increasingly developing and it is sufficient to mention the use of these flavours:

yaourt aux framboises, compare à la framboise
yaourt aux fraises, compare à la fraise.

The leading commercial names in the manufacture of yoghurts are:

Chambourcy,
Danone,
Gervais.

Section B Cheese dishes

Cheese is widely used in the preparation of many dishes. These dishes can appear at various points in the menu, can stand in their own right as a course or can be an adjunct to a principal dish.

Among the more prominent cheese dishes are:

quiche lorraine,
croque-monsieur,
soufflé au fromage,
omelette au fromage,
spaghetti au parmesan,
fondue savoyarde,
crêpe (f) au fromage,
fontainebleau,
fromage blanc à la crème.

Grated cheese is frequently used for 'au gratin' and in the preparation of sauce Mornay.

Exercise 14

1 Name two hard, two cream and two blue French cheeses.
2 At which course would you serve?
  quiche lorraine   soufflé au fromage   bleu de Bresse
  spaghetti au parmesan   petit suisse
3 What do the following terms mean?
  au gratin   plateau de fromages   Mornay   parfumé
  fromages au choix   croque-monsieur
4 Into which category do these cheeses fall?
  cantal   port-salut   roquefort   camembert   petit suisse
  carré de l'est
5 Give three cheeses that may be eaten with sugar.
6 Of the cheeses listed in this Unit, which are not French in origin?

Preparation

1 Collect the names of five different 'yaourts parfumés' by reference to yoghurt cartons.
2 The cheeses mentioned above are manufactured in specific areas of France. Find out which area each cheese is traditionally associated with.

Unit 15

Fruit 1 (les fruits)

Aim: To teach the names of fruit in French
To teach the names of desserts in which fruit is served

It is generally accepted practice that fruit, served as a separate course, appears as the last item on the menu. In this case, it can be presented in several ways:

corbeille de fruits,   ~~basket of fruit~~
fruits de saison,   ~~fruit of season~~
fruits au choix,   ~~Choice of fruit~~

or occasionally as a list of fruit available for that day.

Section A   Individual fruits

The principal fruits are:

la pomme,
la poire,
la banane,
la pêche,
la prune, *plum*
la mirabelle, *small plum*
l'abricot (m),
l'orange (f),
le pamplemousse,
le raisin, *grape*
le citron,
l'ananas (m),
le melon.

The following fruits are generally met in the plural form only:

55

les cerises (f), *cherry —*
les dattes (f),
les figues (f).

The chief soft fruits are:

les fraises (f), *strawberry .*
les framboises (f), *Rasberry.*
les groseilles (f), *redcurrants*
le cassis (m),
les mûres (f). *blackberries*

In addition, nuts may be served as an alternative to fruit as a dessert course:

les amandes (f),
les marrons (m), as in crème de marrons, *chestnuts*
les noisettes (f), *Hazelnuts.*
les noix (f). *walnuts.*

The method of presentation and preparation will, of course, decide at which stage fruit is served. As we have already seen, at the hors-d'oeuvre stage the following may be offered:

pamplemousse rafraîchi, *chilled grapefruit*
melon au porto, *melon in port*
jus d'ananas. *pineapple juice*

As garnishes, the following have also been introduced:

aux amandes,
aux marrons,
with au citron,
à l'orange.

Section B   Preparation of desserts

This section deals with the use of fruit, fruit essences and flavours in the preparation of desserts in various forms.

Stewed fruit is known as 'compote', some examples of which are:

compote de pommes, *stewed apple*
compote d'abricots,
compote de cerises,
compote de figues,
compote de poires.

'Beignets' and 'chaussons' may also have a fruit filling:

beignet de banane, *fritter put in batter Hy.*
beignet de pomme,
beignet d'ananas,
chausson aux pommes. *-apple turnover*

Among the cold sweets using fruit are 'Condé', 'bavarois' and 'coupes'.

abricots Condé — *nice apricots on a bed of sweet me, glazed in juice.*
ananas Condé
pommes Condé
poires Condé

bavarois à la fraise *mixture of sugar egg yolk, milk gelatine*
bavarois à la framboise *and whipped cream.*
bavarois à l'orange
une bavaroise *cream on its own.*

coupe Alexandra *fruit salad kirsh and strawberry ice cream*
coupe pêche Melba *peach vanilla ice cream, cream, raspberry*
coupe poire Belle-Hélène *poach pear ice cream, cream puree*
coupe Jacques *fruit soaked in liquor with various, assorted ices, cumerous + choc sauce*

Section C   Pâtisseries

Fruit is widely used in the preparation of 'bande', 'tarte', 'tartelette' and 'barquette'. Along with other pastry-based items and small cakes, these will appear under the heading 'pâtisseries' on the menu.

Some examples of 'pâtisserie' will be sufficient to show the French usage.

bande aux pommes *strip of pastry.*
tarte aux abricots
barquette aux fraises *boat shape pastry*

Section D   Miscellaneous fruit desserts

There are innumerable desserts in which fruit in one form or other is used. This list gives the more common examples and should be added to as new desserts are met in the course of training.

charlotte aux pommes *breadcrumbs, biscuits*
charlotte aux pêches *line tin on the middle gelatine*
charlotte à l'ananas *or cream + fruit filling on top.*
ananas au kirsch *pineapple slices in kirsh*
bananes flambées
fraises à la crème *strawberry + cream*
fraises rafraîchies *chilled*
poires/pêches au vin rouge/blanc *poast peaches in red wine*
poires au sirop *pears stewed in hot syrup*
pomme bonne-femme *apple served with cream.*
ananas créole *pineapple + rice cream*
prunes à l'eau-de-vie *white spirit - alcohole plum calvados.*
vacherin aux framboises *maringue gata with cream, ice cream + fruit*
vacherin aux fraises
flan à l'orange *orange flan*
salade de fruits *fruit salad*

57

salade d'orange
macédoine de fruits *fruit cocktail with liquer*
pruneaux *dried plum.*

Vocabulary

Masculine		*Feminine*	
beignet	fritter	barquette	'barquette'
bavarois	bavarian cream	bande	tart; slice
cassis	blackcurrant	charlotte	charlotte
chausson	turnover	compote	stewed fruit
Condé	'Condé'	coupe	cup
flan	cream	datte	date
kirsch	'kirsch'	eau-de-vie	brandy, spirit
raisin	grape	figue	fig
sirop	syrup	fraise	strawberry
vacherin	'vacherin'	framboise	raspberry
		groseille	red currant
		mirabelle	mirabelle plum
		mûre	blackberry
		pâtisserie	'pâtisserie'
		prune	plum
		tarte	tart
		tartelette	small tart

Exercise 15

1 Give five ways of serving apple.
2 Give five varieties of 'compote'.
3 With which fruit do you associate the following?
   au kirsch   au vin rouge   créole   au porto   Belle-Hélène
   à l'eau-de-vie
4 Explain the following terms:
   chausson   pâtisserie   vacherin   corbeille   barquette
   bavarois
   Give the gender of each term.
5 Give in French:
   three citrus fruits   three soft fruits   three stone fruits
6 Check back in the book to find which dish these garnishes accompany:
   aux amandes   aux marrons   aux prunes   à l'orange
7 Complete:
   abricots ———   coupe ———   ——— aux pommes
   ——— bonne-femme (a fruit)   charlotte ———
   macédoine de ———

Unit 16

Fruit 2

Aim: **To teach the French for further desserts in which fruit is used**
To give additional conversation practice in ordering a meal

In addition to being served fresh, cooked or as the principal ingredient of a fruit-based dessert, fruit or fruit essence is used as a flavouring for a wide range of sweet dishes, entremets and desserts.

The terms 'au', 'à la', 'aux' figure prominently at this stage and it is essential to have learned the genders of the fruits, in order to use the descriptions correctly.

Here are some of the more usual examples:

Crêpes crêpe au citron *pancakes*
    crêpe à l'orange

Soufflés soufflé à l'orange
    soufflé à l'abricot *steamed*
    soufflé au citron *Pudding* —

Gelées gelée d'orange
    gelée de framboise *jelly*
    gelée de groseille
    gelée de pomme

Mousses mousse au citron
    mousse à la framboise
    mousse à la fraise
    mousse à l'ananas
    compare
    mousse aux framboises
    mousse aux fraises

Glaces glace à l'orange *Ice cream*
    glace au citron
    glace à la fraise
    glace à la framboise
    glace pralinée *powder almond.*
        →*Water Ice.*

Sorbets sorbet à l'orange

Bombes Fruits are rarely mentioned by name in the description of
Iced 'bombes'.
sweat A specialist term, eg
Bomb.
shape.
filled with fruit.

59

bombe au citron
bombe Montmorency (cherry)
bombe tutti frutti (various candied fruits)

is usually given and it is recommended that students compile a personal list, as they come across 'bombes' in the course of their work.

Confitures	confiture d'oranges	_Jam_
	confiture d'abricots	
	confiture de fraises	
	confiture de prunes	
Crèmes	crème à la fraise	
	crème à la framboise	
	compare	
	fraises à la crème	
Savarins	savarin aux fraises	
Flans	flan à l'abricot	
	flan à la fraise	

Various sauces may also have a fruit base, eg
sauce citron
sauce orange

Vocabulary

Masculine		_Feminine_	
flan	a cream	bombe	ice cream dish
savarin	'savarin'	confiture	jam
sorbet	'sorbet'	crème	cream
		crêpe	crepe; pancake
		gelée	jelly
		glace	ice cream
		mousse	'mousse'

Exercise 16

1 Give five desserts in which strawberry is used as a flavouring.
2 What are the following?
   sorbet   crêpe   glace   bombe   praliné

Preparation

By reference to a book of desserts, check the filling of five bombes.

Conversation three

Garçon: Bonsoir madame. Bonsoir monsieur.
Client: Bonsoir monsieur. Deux couverts, s'il vous plaît.
Garçon: Bien monsieur. Par ici.

Garçon: La carte, monsieur, madame.
Client: Merci beaucoup.

Garçon: Vous avez choisi, monsieur?
Client: Moi, je prendrai le melon.
Garçon: Bien. Et pour madame?
Cliente: Je prendrai les oeufs mayonnaise.
Garçon: Qu'est-ce que vous prenez comme viande?
Cliente: Pour moi, le poulet, s'il vous plaît.
Client: Et pour moi, le rôti de veau.
Garçon: Merci beaucoup. Et comme légumes?
Cliente: Les pommes sautées et un peu de salade verte après.
Client: Moi, je prendrai les haricots verts.

1 Practise reading the conversation. Practise the rôles of the three characters.
2 Vary the responses, according to the terms so far studied.
3 Produce a sample menu, in order to simulate restaurant procedures.

Preparation

Draw up the first four courses of an 'à la carte' menu, giving a choice of four to five dishes at each course. Include hors-d'oeuvre, fish, entrée and vegetable.

Pattern practices

1 Je prendrai   le melon
                les tomates
                les olives
                les sardines
                le jambon
2 Qu'est-ce que vous prenez comme viande?
  Pour moi,   le biftek
                le poulet
                le canard
                le veau
                la côtelette de porc
3 Qu'est-ce que vous avez choisi comme légumes?
                les haricots verts   s'il vous plaît
                les petits pois
                les pommes vapeur

Revision test 3 (Units 8 – 12)

1 Potatoes

a) Give the English equivalent for:
pommes chips   pommes frites   pommes nouvelles *n/w*
pommes vapeur   pommes au four *oven*   [5 marks]

b) What have the following methods of preparation in common?
pommes duchesse
pommes marquise

pommes à l'anglaise
pommes vapeur

pommes paille
pommes allumettes

purée de pommes
pommes à la crème
pommes à la neige

pommes rôties
pommes sautées   [5 marks]

What method of preparation is indicated by:

lyonnaise   persillées   en robe des champs *s/p*
mousseline *c/n*   [4 marks]

2 Meat

a) What cuts of meat are the following? Say which meat it is associated with.
épaule *s/p* filet   gigot *l/l*   cuisseau *l/p* selle *s/l* tête
aloyau   carré *o/l* jambe   côtelette   [10 marks]

b) Complete the following meat dishes:
blanquette de ———   escalope de ———
gigot d' ———   filet de ———
rôti de —*v*—   carbon(n)ade de ———   [6 marks]

c) With which dish or cut of meat would you use the following?
au poivre   Rossini   bourguignon   braisé   [4 marks]

d) Give the name of four steaks in French.   [4 marks]

3 Offal (les abats)

a) Give the English for:
foie   rognons   coeur   langue   tripes   [5 marks]

b) Give the gender of each item. [5 marks]

c) With which of the above would you expect to see the following terms?

à la mode de Caen 🖝   à la broche 🖝   braisé   farci   [4 marks]

4 Eggs

a) Give the English equivalent of the following preparations:

sur le plat   durs 🖝   brouillés 🖝   farcis   à la coque
pochés   mollets [7 marks]

b) Give the preparation of these omelettes.

nature   au fromage   au jambon   aux champignons
espagnole [5 marks]

5 Game (gibier)

a) What is the English for?

lapin   lièvre   canard   faisan   caille   caneton [6 marks]

b) Complete the following preparations:

civet de ———   ——— à l'orange   sauté de ———
——— rôti   ——— au vin [5 marks]

75 marks

Unit 17

Desserts (les desserts)

Aim: To teach the names of further desserts using flavours which are not fruit based

So far we have looked only at those desserts associated with fruits. Many desserts have flavours other than those given in Units 15 and 16. This particularly applies to

crêpes,
glaces,
soufflés,
crèmes.

Common flavours are

>au chocolat
>au café
>au rhum
>au moka
>à l'eau-de-vie
>à la vanille

crêpes

>crêpe au rhum
>crêpe à la confiture (d'abricots) Jam
>crêpe Suzette orange brandy.
>crêpe au beurre
>crêpe au sucre
>crêpe au Grand Marnier*
>crêpe au kirsch*
>* or almost any liqueur
>cf Unit 27

soufflés

>soufflé au café
>soufflé au chocolat
>soufflé à la vanille

omelettes soufflées

>omelette soufflée à l'orange
>omelette soufflée au citron
>omelette soufflée au Cointreau (or other liqueur)

mousses

>mousse au café
>mousse au chocolat
>mousse au moka

glaces

>glace au café
>glace au chocolat
>glace à la vanille

crèmes

>crème caramel
>crème au café
>crème renversée caramel custard
>crème anglaise
>crème à la vanille

64

petits pots de crème
crème Chantilly — *Whipped cream + sugar*
crème brûlée — *Burnt Brown Sugar.*
crème bavaroise au café
bavarois au café
bavarois au chocolat
crème bavaroise au chocolat

(NB Not all the 'crèmes' given here are served as a dessert in their own right. Some are an accompaniment.)

flans
French Custard tart
flan au café
flan au caramel
flan à la vanille
flan à la pistache

As well as the 'beignets', 'crêpes' and 'pâtisseries' met in this and the preceding unit, a good many other desserts are based on a pastry or dough mixture with an appropriate flavouring. Among the more well-known desserts are:

éclair au chocolat,
éclair au café,
profiteroles au chocolat,
choux à la crème,
baba au rhum,
baba flambé,
savarin au rhum,
savarin Chantilly,
savarin à la crème,
cornets à la crème.

Miscellaneous desserts include:

gâteau,
riz à l'impératrice,
gâteau de riz,
meringues glacées,
omelette surprise à l'orange,
omelette surprise aux fruits panachés,
omelette norvégienne,
oeufs à la neige,
île flottante,
crème de marrons,
sabayon au marsala,
bûche de Noël,
mille-feuille,
pithiviers.

'Gâteaux secs' may also be served as a dessert or as an accompaniment. The more common ones are:

> palmiers,
> langues de chat,
> tuiles aux amandes,
> éventail.

Vocabulary

Masculine		*Feminine*	
baba	'baba'	bûche (de Noël)	log
café	coffee	eau-de-vie	brandy, spirit
caramel	caramel	meringue	meringue
chocolat	chocolate	pâtisserie	'pâtisserie'
cornet	horn	pistache	pistachio
éclair	éclair	profiterole	'profiterole'
éventail	fan	vanille	vanilla
flan	a cream	tuile	'tile'
gâteau	cake		
Grand Marnier	a liqueur		
liqueur	liqueur		
moka	mocha		
rhum	rum		
sabayon	'sabayon'		
savarin	'savarin'		
soufflé	'soufflé'		
marsala	dessert wine		

Exercise 17

1 Give five flavourings for dessert dishes not based on fruit.
2 Find five separate desserts which could be served:
   au café,
   au chocolat.
   (NB A dessert may equally well have both flavours.)
3 Name the three liqueurs used as flavours mentioned in this Unit.
4 Distinguish between the following:
   omelette surprise   omelette soufflée   soufflé
   Make reference to a good cookery book, if in doubt.
5 What desserts would you associate with the following terms:
   au rhum   Suzette   brûlée   au marsala   à l'impératrice
6 Complete the following, restricting your answers to this Unit:
   ——— de Noël   ——— flambé   ——— glacées
   éclair ———   glace à la ———
7 From the list of 'crèmes' given in this Unit, list those which are used as an accompaniment to a main preparation.

66

8 Explain the following terms:

flambé   Chantilly   panaché   gâteaux secs   pithiviers

Aural comprehension 3

Listen carefully to the short snatches of conversation read to you. Answer the questions set out below, a), b), c) or d), according to which you think is the most appropriate answer to each question.

1 Which course do you think the waiter was enquiring about?

a) hors-d'oeuvre   c) légumes
b) poisson   d) entrée

2 Which course is in question in this conversation?

a) entrée   c) poisson
b) légumes   d) hors-d'oeuvre

3 What is the principal ingredient of the soup?

a) cauliflower   c) potatoes
b) carrots   d) It isn't a vegetable soup.

4 Did the customer order?

a) chicken   c) pork
b) beef   d) lamb

5 What was the customer's order?

a) fish   c) beef
b) lamb   d) pork

6 The customer has just ordered the entrée. What could the only logical answer be?

a) tomato salad   c) green salad
b) Russian salad   d) cucumber salad

7 For dessert did the customer choose?

a) fruit   c) pastry
b) ice cream   d) soufflé

8 Did the customer prefer?

a) oranges   c) apple
b) apricots   d) plum

9 Did the customer order?

a) cheese   c) pastry
b) ice cream   d) fruit

10 What sort of cheese was ordered?

a) blue   c) semi-hard
b) hard   d) cream

Unit 18

Sauces (les sauces)

Aim: To teach the French terms associated with making sauces
To introduce the names of a selection of sauces

The terms associated with sauces and allied garnishes need very careful understanding before they can be handled with accuracy and confidence. These terms are met very early on in a catering course and it would obviously be very helpful for students to have reference to this Unit throughout their course. At this stage, however, it will serve as a useful revision and put some order into an area of catering which may be only partly understood. It can also help to fill in any gaps that have been left during the course of the year's work.

Fonds de cuisine

Basic to most sauces, other than butter based sauces, are the 'fonds' or 'fonds de cuisine'. These are: *basic stock*

fond blanc, *white stock*
fond brun (estouffade), *brown stock* *basic (slow stewing)*
fond de volaille, *chicken*
fond de gibier, *game*
fumet, *smoked. light essence*
fumet de poisson. *light essence of fish*

Glaces

These fonds are used to make 'glaces' or 'demi-glaces': *glaze = meat juice.*

glace de viande (boeuf, veau, porc, mouton), *from meat*
glace de volaille, *poultry*
glace de poisson, *fish*
glace de gibier. *game.*

Liaisons

Various liaisons are used to thicken or bind the 'fonds' to produce sauces. The main liaisons are:

beurre manié, *butter + flour - thickening (kneaded)*
jaune d'oeuf, *egg yolk*

68

crème,
crème et jaune d'oeuf, *cream + egg yolk*
fécule, *Potatoe starch.*
roux   roux blanc, *white roux.*
        roux blònd,
        roux brun (espagnole). *brown (foundation of demi glace) added to stock.*

The basic sauce

Excluding egg and butter sauces, there are five basic sauces from which all other sauces, whatever their special flavour, are derived:

espagnole, *brown stock foundation demiglace*
demi-glace,
jus lié, *thickend gravy arrowroot*
béchamel, *basic white sauce*
velouté. *chicken or fish thick white sauce. Stock and milk*

In order to simplify learning the names of sauces, they have been separated into three groups.

Group A includes those sauces where the main ingredient is obvious from the name eg sauce moutarde.
Group B includes sauces whose descriptive term derives from the name of a town, country, region or person.
Group C must be learned by reference to the name itself.

There are several alternative classifications of sauces,
eg sauces blondes,
    sauces brunes,
    sauces chaudes,
    sauces froides,
but for the student of French it is perhaps easier to tackle them by reference to terms already known.

Group A

Sauces where the principal ingredient or flavour is given by name.

Sauce	Example of use
sauce anchois	Darne de cabillaud sauce anchois
sauce moutarde	Harengs grillés sauce moutarde
sauce câpre	Filet de sole poché sauce câpre
sauce madère	Jambon braisé sauce madère
sauce champignon	Escalope de veau sauce champignon
sauce raifort	Rôti de boeuf sauce raifort *Horseradish.*
sauce menthe	Gigot d'agneau sauce menthe (not standard French accompaniment)
sauce homard	Filet de sole poché sauce homard

Sauce	*Example of use*
sauce persil	
sauce tomate	
sauce à la crème	

Group B

Sauces associated with place names.

		[handwritten]
sauce béarnaise	Filet de boeuf sauce béarnaise	[hollandaise + tarragon]
sauce hollandaise	Filet de sole sauce hollandaise	[yolks of egg + butter]
sauce lyonnaise	Sauté de foie sauce lyonnaise	[onion egg yolk white wine]
sauce hongroise	Escalope de veau sauce hongroise	[onion parsley fry in butter]
sauce normande	[liason (eggs + cream)]	
sauce bordelaise	Filet de boeuf sauce bordelaise	[demi glace red wine thyme + bayleaf]
sauce provençale	[chopped tomatoes garlic oil shallots olive.]	
sauce Périgueux	[truffel in a madeira sauce]	
sauce Bercy	Filet de sole sauce Bercy	[white wine fish velouté]

[handwritten] [½ glace vinegar reduction.]

Group C

Sauces where the principal flavour or ingredient is recognised by the name only.

[handwritten heading] [white sauce + tomato flavour]

		[handwritten]
sauce Aurore	Suprêmes de volaille pochés sauce Aurore	
sauce Robert	Côtelettes de porc sauce Robert	[½ glace white wine vinegar + chopped onion + mustard]
sauce Soubise	Côtelettes d'agneau sauce Soubise	[onion] [white sauce]
sauce Réforme	Côtelettes d'agneau sauce Réforme	[egg white + cayenne buttered eggs butter lemon juice flour] [demi glace]
sauce Mornay	Filet de sole sauce Mornay	[cheese sauce bechamal.]
sauce cardinal	Filet de sole poché sauce cardinal	[bechamal sauce fish stock truffle essence lobster butter cayenne]
sauce chasseur	Poulet sauté sauce chasseur	[white wine shallots white wine - demi glace pepper]
sauce diable	Entrecôte grillée sauce diable	[shallots pepper white reduced - cayenne pepper]
sauce piquante	Côtelette de porc sauce piquante	[demi glace white wine vinegar herbs onions]
sauce meunière	[noisette butter lemon juice parsley]	
sauce Chateaubriand	Filet de boeuf sauce Chateaubriand	[chopped shallots thyme mushrooms white wine demi glace + butter]
sauce suprême	[chicken velouté]	
sauce mayonnaise		
sauce vinaigrette		
sauce tartare	Filet de sole sauce tartare	[capers gherkins parsley mayonnaise]
sauce Duxelles	[chopped mushroom shallots in butter]	
sauce bigarade	Caneton braisé sauce bigarade	[orange + lemon juice.]

These lists are of course by no means complete nor is it possible to indicate a complete range of dishes to which the various sauces are added. This is a question of experience and practice. Students should continue to compile their own lists as they come across new sauces in the course of their training.

Exercise 18

1 Name five different 'fonds de cuisine'.
2 Name five 'liaisons'.
3 What are the following items?
   glace (in terms of this unit)   estouffade   fumet   roux
   espagnole
4 With which dishes would you expect to serve the following sauces?
   sauce madère   sauce moutarde   sauce raifort   sauce câpre
   sauce champignon
5 With what would you expect to serve?
   sauce lyonnaise   sauce bordelaise   sauce Bercy   sauce hongroise
   sauce béarnaise
6 Give a dish to accompany the following sauces?
   sauce Robert   sauce chasseur   sauce diable   sauce piquante
   sauce bigarade

Preparation

1 By reference to a good cookery book, find out the principal dishes these
   sauces might accompany.
   sauce Réforme   sauce Soubise   sauce Périgueux
   sauce provençale   sauce Duxelles

Unit 19

Sauces and garnishes

**Aim: To give further practice in handling the names of sauces
         To revise descriptive terms for sauces and garnishes**

In Unit 18 we saw that sauces, in addition to having the main flavour
clearly stated, may be designated either by reference to a region, town,
country or person or by a name which indicates the principal flavour.

Section A   Sauces

By reference to a good cookery book or recipe book, verify the principal
ingredients and/or flavour of the following sauces and list dishes which they
could accompany.

béarnaise
hollandaise
lyonnaise
hongroise
normande
bordelaise
provençale
Périgueux
Bercy

Similarly, identify the principal flavour of these sauces and list any dishes they might accompany.

Aurore
Robert
Soubise
Réforme
Mornay
cardinal
chasseur
diable
piquante
meunière
Chateaubriand
suprême
mayonnaise
vinaigrette
tartare
Duxelles
bigarade

Section B   Garnishes

Main course dishes (grillades, rôtis, entrées) and fish dishes sometimes have the vegetable garnish indicated as an integral part of the dish. Students will find it valuable to verify the composition of such garnishes, which are indicated by a simple descriptive phrase or appellation. Some have already been introduced in preceding Units and others will be recognizable by reference to dishes served at previous courses. The purpose of this Unit is to draw this information together for easy reference and revision.

Using a good set of cookery books, check the composition of the following garnishes. The first group is associated with meat or poultry dishes.

Group A

boulangère POTATOES
bruxelloise BRAISED CHICKORY BRUSSEL SPROUTS
Clamart   PEAS
Du Barry   CALIFLOWER

72

fermière MIX VEG
florentine SPINACH.
jardinière SPRING VEG
Judic
Parmentier POTATOES
portugaise TOMATO's
printanière SPRING VEG
provençale TOMATOE, GALIC OLIVE OIL ONIONS
Duxelles CHOPPED MUSHROOM
Rossini LIVER PATE TRUFFLES
pré-salé ⎱ These are used in conjunction
vert-pré ⎰ with lamb only

Group B
The following group is associated with fish dishes:

bonne femme house wife style
Véronique
dieppoise shimps, Mussels, Mushrooms.
belle-meunière COOKED IN BUTTER
marinière shalots, parsley, white wine, Butter.
Doria CUCUMBER
armoricaine

Group C
Miscellaneous

niçoise BLACK OLIVES ANCHOVIES. GREEN BEAN.
milanaise spagetti TOMATE SAUCE, CHEESE, HAM, TRUFFLES.
indienne Spice, CURRY.

The following garnishes are in common use but fall outside the classifications given so far. A few have also been met at other points in the course.

au beurre noir BURNT BUTTER
au beurre maître d'hôtel CHOPPED parsley/lemon Juice
au beurre noisette
aux croûtons
aux fines herbes
royale egg Custard.

Finally it would be useful to add to this Unit a series of miscellaneous terms frequently met in the process of preparation and serving, which might otherwise be omitted,

court-bouillon (m)
bouquet garni (m)
chapelure (f)
brunoise (f)
mirepoix (f)

as well as these terms used in the preparation of vegetables:

jardinière,
julienne,
printanière,
compare potages, using these terms.

Exercise 19

1 Re-classify the sauces already introduced, according to the following headings:
Cold sauces   Egg-based sauces   Sauces based on demi-glace
Sauces based on béchamel   Sauces used only with fish dishes

Preparation

Compile, with the aid of a good set of cookery books, dishes with which the garnishes given in this Unit could be used.

Unit 20

Methods of preparation: a glossary of terms

Aim: To revise various methods of preparation or service

The following glossary of terms includes the main methods of preparing and serving dishes and gives examples of their use. Although a good number have already been introduced, the Unit serves as a useful revision and reference point.

The first group comprises terms which may appear on the menu itself.

bouilli	boeuf bouilli
braisé	boeuf braisé, oignons braisés
farci	tomates farcies, poivrons farcis
fouetté	crème fouettée
flambé	banane flambée
fricassé	fricassée de boeuf
frit	filets de sole frits, scampi frits
fumé	saumon fumé
grillé	steak grillé

haché	viande hachée
panaché	glace panachée
pané	escalope de veau panée
poché	darne de cabillaud pochée
poêlé	escalope poêlée
praliné	glace pralinée
rafraîchi	fraises rafraîchies
râpé	carottes râpées
rôti	faisan rôti
sauté	pommes sautées

The second group refer to terms more descriptive of preparation or service.

concassé	tomates concassées
arrosé	arrosé de cognac, café arrosé
chambré	vin rouge chambré
frappé	champagne frappé

Exercise 20

In all these exercises pay special attention to agreements.

1 Use the following preparations in an hors-d'oeuvre:
   râpé   farci   fumé   *Carotte rapé tomatos farci   Saurci fumo*

2 Use the following methods of preparation in connection with fish dishes:
   poché   frit   grillé

3 Use the following terms in the preparation of vegetable dishes:
   braisé   sauté   farci   bouilli

4 Suggest dessert dishes which might be served:
   rafraîchi   fouetté   praliné   poché   flambé

5 Add an appropriate method of service to the following:
   entrecôte   artichauts   escalope de veau   chou   framboises

6 In this case, the agreements are given. Complete correctly:
   ———— grillées   ———— râpé   ———— sautées   ———— pochés
   ———— panées

Aural comprehension 4

Listen carefully to the items read out to you. After each sentence has been read, answer the question set on it, a), b), c) or d), according to which you think is the correct answer.

1 Which sauce is the most likely to accompany the dish read out?
   a) mayonnaise   c) béarnaise
   b) anchois   d) normande

2 What is the principal flavouring of the sauce read out?
   a) onion   c) lobster
   b) truffles   d) egg

3 Which dish is the sauce read out most likely to accompany?
a) côtelette d'agneau   c) filet de sole
b) Chateaubriand   d). goujon de plie

4 Which sauce could be an alternative to the sauce read out?
a) sauce bordelaise   c) sauce madère
b) sauce hongroise   d) sauce à l'orange

5 With which course would the sauce be served?
a) fish   c) meat
b) hors-d'oeuvre   d) vegetable

6 Would you expect this sauce to be served with?
a) artichokes   c) kidneys
b) ice cream   d) peaches

7 What would the most appropriate accompaniment to this dish be?
a) Grand Marnier   c) chasseur
b) Mornay   d) hollandaise

8 What is the main flavouring in the garnish mentioned?
a) cauliflower   c) egg
b) peas   d) grapes

9 How would you expect this to be served?
a) fouetté   c) frappé
b) flambé   d) farci

10 Would you expect to hear this description with?
a) ice cream   c) biscuits
b) potatoes   d) fish

Unit 21

Condiments, herbs and spices

Aim: To teach the French for various flavouring agents

The use of seasonings, herbs, spices and various flavourings adds distinction to the dishes they accompany without detracting from the main ingredients, which they should enhance. They are widely incorporated in cooking at all stages but their use varies very much from dish to dish and from country to country.

It will be noted that certain herbs, sage and mint for example, are very popular in the United Kingdom, while a flavouring like curry which appears in oriental dishes has very wide appeal. On the other hand, garlic, basil, rosemary and fennel are much more typical of Provençal cooking. Paprika is associated with Hungarian dishes.

In this Unit the principal herbs, spices and seasonings are given and an indication of their use, where appropriate, is added to give examples of their application to French cuisine.

Section A

Condiments

sel (m)	sel ~~salt~~	
	sel de mer ~~sea salt~~	
	sel de céleri ~~celery salt~~	
	sel d'ail	
poivre (m) ~~Pepper~~	poivre gris	Steak au poivre
	poivre de Cayenne	Saucisson au poivre
	paprika	Sauce hongroise
moutarde (f)	moutarde	Hareng grillé sauce moutarde
	moutarde de Dijon (Commercial names are Grey-Poupon, Amora, Maille)	

Herbes

ciboulette (f)	salad garnish ~~chives~~	
feuilles de laurier	bouquet garni ~~bayleaf~~	
persil (m)	bouquet garni fines herbes ~~Parsley~~	
menthe (f)		Sauce menthe (predominantly British)
sauge (f) ~~sage~~		
thym (m)	bouquet garni	
romarin (m) ~~rosemary~~		Poisson grillé au romarin
		Poulet rôti au romarin
		Rôti de veau au romarin
fenouil (m) ~~fennel~~	court-bouillon (fish)	Grillade aux fenouils
		Fenouils braisés
fines herbes		Omelette aux fines herbes
persil		
cerfeuil (m) ~~chervil~~		
estragon (m) ~~tarragon~~		
ciboulette ~~chives~~		
estragon	sauce béarnaise	Daube de veau à l'estragon
basilic (m)	soupe au pistou	

Épices (f)

Épices (f)		Pain d'épices
cari (curry) (m)		Sauce indienne
clou de girofle ~~cloves~~	mixed spice	Oignon clouté

cannelle (f) *cinnamon*　　　　　　　　　　Crème à la cannelle
noix muscade *nutmeg*
safran (m)　　　　　bouillabaisse　　　　　Riz au safran
safron

Miscellaneous
ail　　　*garlic*　　　　　　　　　　　　Saucisson à l'ail
piment (m) *pimento*　　　　　　　　　...... aux piments
　　　　　　　　　　　　　　　　　　(as a garnish)
poivron (m) *peppers*　　　　　　　　　Poivrons farcis
huile　*oil*　　　huile d'olive　*olive*
　　　　　　　huile d'arachide　*nut oil*
　　　　　　　huile de maïs　*maize/corn*
　　　　　　　huile de tournesol　*sunflower*
cèpe (m) ceps (m) *mushrooms*　　　　　Omelettes aux cèpes
truffe (f) *truffle* sauce Périgueux　　　Pâté de foie truffé
seigle (m)　*rye*　　　　　　　　　　　Pain de seigle
lait (m)　　*milk*　　　　*bread* Pain au lait

Sweet flavourings
miel (m)　*honey*　　　　　　　　　　Crêpes au miel
confiture (f)　*jam*　　　　　　　　　Crêpe à la confiture

Section B

Infusions (tisanes)
thé (m)　*tea*　　　　　　　　　　　Thé nature　*natural*
thé de Chine　*china tea*　　　　　　Thé citron　*lemon*
tilleul (m)　*lime*
verveine (f)　*verbena*
camomille (f)　*commamile*

Vocabulary

Masculine		*Feminine*	
basilic	basil	camomille	camomile
cari (curry)	curry	cannelle	cinnamon
cèpe	small mushroom	ciboulette	chive
cerfeuil	chervil	feuille	leaf
clou de girofle	clove	menthe	mint
estragon	tarragon	moutarde	mustard
lait	milk	noix muscade	nutmeg
laurier	bay	sauge	sage
miel	honey	tisane	infusion
paprika	paprika	truffe	truffle
persil	parsley	verveine	verbena
piment	pimento		
poivre	pepper (ground)		
poivron	pepper		

78

Masculine

romarin	rosemary
safran	saffron
seigle	rye
sel	salt
tilleul	lime
thé	tea
thym	thyme
tournesol	sunflower

Exercise 21

Answer the following questions, a), b), c) according to which you think is the correct answer.

1 Moutarde de Dijon comes from
  a) the Dijon region.
  b) Maille.
  c) Grey-Poupon.

2 Sauce hongroise will include
  a) poivre gris.
  b) poivre de Cayenne.
  c) paprika.

3 How would you expect steak to be served?
  a) cannelle
  b) au poivre
  c) au lait

4 Which herb would you expect in a bouquet garni?
  a) sauge
  b) menthe
  c) thym

5 In a fish court-bouillon would you expect?
  a) estragon
  b) poivron
  c) fenouil

6 Which may be served as a vegetable in its own right?
  a) fenouil
  b) basilic
  c) romarin

7 Which herb is a member of the onion family?
  a) ciboulette
  b) romarin
  c) basilic

8 Which *two* herbs feature in 'fines herbes'?
  a) estragon et menthe
  b) cerfeuil et persil
  c) ciboulette et romarin

9 Which herb is particularly used in roast?
   a) menthe
   b) piment
   c) romarin
10 Which would you expect in a 'bouquet garni'?
   a) feuilles de laurier
   b) fenouil
   c) estragon
11 Which herb is used in sauce béarnaise?
   a) basilic
   b) estragon
   c) fenouil
12 Sauce indienne would contain
   a) curry,
   b) estragon,
   c) clou de girofle.
13 Which spice gives a yellow colour?
   a) safran
   b) piment
   c) noix muscade
14 Which is the ground-nut oil?
   a) huile d'olive
   b) huile de maïs
   c) huile d'arachide
15 Which is the odd one out?
   a) cèpe
   b) truffe
   c) seigle
16 What would you expect as the principal flavouring in a 'sauce Périgueux'?
   a) cèpe
   b) truffe
   c) lait
17 With what would an onion be studded?
   a) cari
   b) clou de girofle
   c) huile d'arachide
18 'Au miel' would garnish
   a) saucisson
   b) pâté de foie
   c) crêpe
19 With what would you make an 'infusion'?
   a) sucre
   b) miel
   c) verveine
20 'Tilleul' is
   a) a tisane,
   b) a herb,
   c) a spice.

Unit 22

La batterie de cuisine

Aim: **To teach the more usual terms associated with**
la batterie de cuisine and la brigade de cuisine

La batterie de cuisine

This term is used to indicate the various small utensils used in the kitchen.
The main items are:

la casserole, *steamer*
le bain-marie, *water bath*
la marmite, *steamer stock pot*
la poêle (à frire), *frying pan*
la sauteuse. *deep frying pan. shallow*

The items used in the preparation and service of food are:

le chinois, *conical strainer*
le couteau, *knife*
la cuiller (la cuillère), *spoon*
le fouet, *whisk*
la fourchette, *fork*
la louche, *ladel*
la passoire, *strainer*
la râpe, *grater*
le rouleau, *rolling pin*
le tamis. *sieve*

The principal items of chinaware are:

l'assiette (f), *meat plate*
l'assiette creuse, *soup plate*
le bol, *bowl*
la soucoupe, *saucer*
la tasse. *cup*

Other useful items of kitchenware are:

les ciseaux (pl) (m), *scissors*
l'ouvre-boîte (m), *can opener*
le tire-bouchon, *cork screw*
le torchon. *cloth*

The items of household equipment associated with the kitchen are:

le congélateur,
la cuisinière électrique,
à gaz,
le four,
le gril,
le lave-vaisselle,
le réfrigérateur (le frigidaire, le frigo).

La brigade de cuisine

This term is applied to include all members of the kitchen staff. In relatively large restaurants, each member of the team is employed but frequently many functions are carried out by the same member of staff. The main members of the 'brigade' are:

le chef de cuisine,
le sous-chef,
le chef de partie,
  eg le chef pâtissier,
     le chef rôtisseur,
     le chef saucier,
l'entremettier,
le sommelier.

Junior members of the team are:

le commis,
l'apprenti (e).

The 'aboyeur' is the link between the restaurant dining-room and the kitchens. In the dining-room there will be a maître d'hôtel and one or more serveur or serveuse.

Vocabulary

Masculine		Feminine	
aboyeur	barker	batterie	battery
apprenti	apprentice	brigade	staff, team
bain-marie	'bain-marie'	cuiller ⎫	spoon
bol	bowl	cuillère ⎭	
chef de cuisine	chef	cuisinière	cooker, stove
chef de partie	section chef	électricité	electricity
chinois	conical strainer	fourchette	fork
les ciseaux	scissors	louche	ladle
congélateur	freezer	partie	section
commis	assistant	passoire	strainer, sieve
couteau	knife	râpe	grater

82

Masculine		Feminine	
entremettier	vegetable cook	sauteuse	frying-pan
fouet	whisk	serveuse	waitress
four	oven	soucoupe	saucer
gaz	gas		
gril	grill		
maître d'hôtel	head waiter		
lave-vaisselle	dish-washer		
pâtissier	pastry-cook		
ouvre-boîte	tin-opener		
réfrigérateur	refrigerator		
rôtisseur	roasting chef		
rouleau	rolling pin		
saucier	sauce chef		
serveur	waiter		
sommelier	wine-waiter		
sous-chef	second chef		
tamis	tammy cloth, strainer		
tire-bouchon	cork screw		
torchon	cloth		

Exercise 22

1 These terms have already appeared in previous Units. Complete:
———— à la poêle ———— marmite assiette ————
———— en tasse ———— au four
2 At which stage in the meal would the dishes in question 1 be served?
3 Explain:
commis chinois congélateur 'partie' entremetteur
Give the gender of each.
4 Complete:
bain ———— brigade de ———— ———— rôtisseur
maître ———— cuisinière à ————
5 a) Associate another culinary term with the word given,
eg sauteuse: sauté
râpe fouet poêle gril pâtissier
b) Using the new words, add a second word to make a culinary term,
eg sauté: pommes sautées
6 For the preparation of what dishes would you use:
bain-marie tamis chinois

Revision test 4 (Units 13 – 21)

1 Volaille

a) Give the English for the following:
le poulet   le caneton   le canard   le dindon
l'oie   [5 marks]

b) Explain the following terms with reference to 'volaille'.
suprêmes de volaille   poulet de grain   ballottines
de Bresse   chasseur   [5 marks]

c) Complete:
———— en cocotte   ———— à l'orange
———— farci aux marrons   ———— au vin
———— sauté provençale   [5 marks]

2 Les fromages

a) Give a French cheese which is:
a hard cheese   a semi-hard cheese   a cream cheese
a blue cheese   a dish in which cheese is the main
ingredient   [5 marks]

b) Explain the terms:
plateau de fromages   fromage de chèvre   yaourt nature
Chambourcy   Mornay   [5 marks]

3 Les fruits

a) What have the following pairs of fruits in common?
pommes, poires   citron, orange   pêche, prune
fraises, framboises   amandes, marrons   [5 marks]

b) Complete:
———— frappé   corbeille de ————
———— Condé   ———— aux abricots
———— au kirsch   [5 marks]

c) What are?
beignets   compote   chausson   barquette
bavarois   [5 marks]
Name a different fruit associated with each item above   [5 marks]

d) Complete using a different fruit at each stage:
crêpe ————   mousse ————   confiture ————
sorbet ————   glace ————   [5 marks]

4 Desserts

a) Complete:
——— au chocolat ——— à la confiture
——— au rhum profiteroles ———
riz ——— [5 marks]

5 Les sauces

a) Explain the following terms:
glace de volaille estouffade espagnole Béchamel
sauce madère [5 marks]

b) Give a dish which the following sauces would accompany
sauce moutarde sauce béarnaise sauce Bercy
sauce Réforme sauce piquante [5 marks]

c) Give the principal flavouring in:
sauce lyonnaise sauce Périgueux sauce Aurore
Duxelles Rossini [5 marks]

6 Condiments, etc

a) With what do you associate the following? Complete the terms.
——— au poivre ——— aux fines herbes
——— au miel ——— truffé
——— aux fenouils [5 marks]

b) To what use would you put the following?
romarin estragon ail cèpes tilleul [5 marks]

80 marks

Unit 23

Wines of France (les vins de France)

Aim: To introduce vocabulary and terms allied to the French wine industry

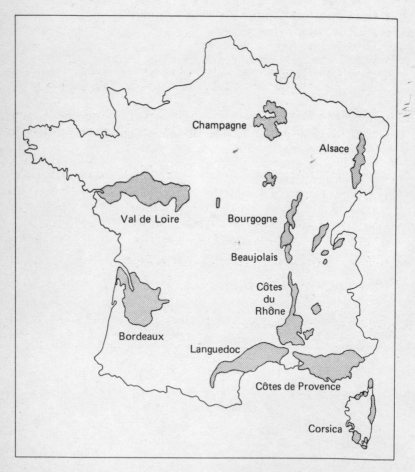

When dealing with 'Les vins de France', it is extremely difficult within the space of four units to do justice to the wealth of knowledge and mystique which appertains to this specialized branch of catering.

Wine drinking is, in the last analysis, a question of personal preference but the more you know about a subject, the more certain you become of the reasons for your preference and the more confident you are in handling situations where your judgement is required. The student should bear in mind that this brief introduction will not make a wine connoisseur nor even a wine waiter, although it may stimulate an interest to develop a specialist knowledge, which could provide an additional qualification to offer a prospective employer.

This section is written with a certain humility in the full realization that it can only serve as an introduction, but it will provide a passable knowledge of the usual range of wines available, their individual qualities and origins and help to dispel some of that mystery which surrounds the subject.

Section A   Classification of wines

The majority of French wines are:

vin rouge,
vin blanc,
vin rosé,
champagne,
vin mousseux.   *soft wine - sweet*

Depending on their region of production, the quantity and quality produced, and geographical and geological features, like climate, soil or drainage, they are classified as:

château bottled, *Everything done in one place*
appellation contrôlée, *quality controller*
VDQS (vins délimités de qualité supérieure), *top class wine*
'vin de pays', *country wine - not top quality*
vin ordinaire or vin de table, *table wine*
'carafe' wine. *carafe of wine*

Section B   Wine producing areas of France

The chief wine producing areas of France are:

Champagne,
Alsace,
Val de Loire,
Bourgogne,
Beaujolais,
Côtes du Rhône,
Bordeaux,
Côtes de Provence,
Languedoc.

Section C Bottles

The shape of the bottle in which the wine is kept is to a certain extent an indication of the origin of the wine.

Bordeaux   Bourgogne   Alsace   Champagne

It is customary to order wine by the bottle, or in the case of cheap wines already decanted, by the 'carafe'. The terms in use are:

> la bouteille,
> la demi-bouteille,
> la carafe,
> un demi de blanc, de rouge (litre is understood),
> un quart de blanc, etc (litre is again understood).

It is known in certain establishments to serve wine by the glass – le verre.

Section D Glasses

Good glasses enhance the appearance of wine and the tulip shape helps to concentrate the 'bouquet'. Wine may be served in glasses which have a specialized shape specifically of the wine in question:

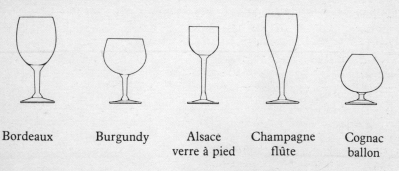

Bordeaux   Burgundy   Alsace   Champagne   Cognac
                            verre à pied   flûte   ballon

Service of wines

Red wines should ideally be served 'chambré'; white wines and rosé should be served 'frais'; champagne and 'vins liquoreux' frappés.

Section E   Allied vocabulary

The following terms are in common use in connection with various aspects of the wine trade and should therefore be known:

mis en bouteille,   *put in bottle*
mis en bouteille au château (vins de Bordeaux),
mis en bouteille   au domaine   *region*
                à la propriété (vins de Bourgogne, in particular),
                by proprietor
grand cru,
premier cru,
cuvée,
Côtes de ......,
clos,
pétillant,
sec/doux.

Section F   Main types of grape

All manner of conditions give rise to the very variable nature of wine, not only from place to place but from year to year, and at times from vineyard to vineyard.

However, there is some consistency in the vines grown in the various districts of France and these are the main grapes according to region:

Grapes	Principal area
Gamay	Beaujolais
Sauvignon Blanc	Bordeaux — Graves et Sauternes
Pinot Blanc	Champagne
Pinot Noir	Bourgogne et Champagne
Sylvaner	Alsace
Chardonnay	Chablis
Traminer	Alsace
Riesling	Alsace
Cabernet Sauvignon	Bordeaux
Chenin Blanc	Loire Valley
Grenache	Rhône Valley

Vocabulary

Masculine		Feminine	
ballon	'ballon'	appellation	name
château	castle	bouteille	bottle

Masculine		Feminine	
cru	vintage	carafe	carafe
domaine	domain	côte	hillside
clos	vineyard	cuvée	vat, barrel
litre	litre	flûte	flute glass
pays	country	demi-bouteille	half bottle
verre	glass	mise en bouteille	bottling process
vin	wine	propriété	domain
		table	table
		tulipe	tulip glass

Exercise 23

1 What is the meaning of the following expressions?
vin mousseux   vin de pays   une carafe   une flûte   sec

2 The following expressions could all be seen on the label of a bottle. What do they mean or imply?
appellation contrôlée   VDQS   premier cru   mis en bouteille
Côtes du Rhône

3 Which grape is used in the production of?
chablis   white wine of the Loire
Which grape is particularly associated with?
champagne   Rhône wines, especially rosé   graves and sauternes

4 Which wines do you associate with these bottles?

5 Working north to south down the Saône-Rhône Valley, list the five main wine producing are as mentioned in this Unit.

6 Which wine would you expect to be served in these glasses?

90

Unit 24

Wines of France –
Alsace and Loire Valley

Aim: **To introduce the wines of Champagne, Alsace, the Loire Valley**
To practise conversations involving ordering wine
To teach the use of 'de'

In this unit we shall look at wines produced in some of the regions of France mentioned in the previous Unit. The wines dealt with will be wines of quality ie château bottled, appellation contrôlée or VDQS wines. Little need be said about 'vins de pays' or 'vins ordinaires', except that they are considerably cheaper because they lack the qualities of the nobler wines.

Champagne

This is a sparkling white wine of very great reputation produced in the Champagne district of France, centred on Reims (Rheims, in English). It is blended from the juice of the Pinot Noir, Pinot Blanc and Chardonnay grapes. There are three main grape growing areas:

> Montagne de Reims (black grapes) in the north of the region,
> Vallée de la Marne (black grapes) in the centre,
> Côtes de Blanc (white grapes) in the south of the region.

According to the degree of sweetness, champagnes are:

> brut,
> sec,
> demi-sec,
> riche (the sweetest).

Champagne made from white grapes only is known as

> blanc de blancs.

Some of the best known firms supplying champagne are:

> Charles Heidsieck,
> Krug,
> Mercier,
> Moët et Chandon,
> Pol Roger,

Pommery et Greno,
Ruinart,
Taittinger,
Veuve Clicquot.

These are the 'grandes marques'.

Champagne is best served 'frappé' in a 'flûte'.

Vins d'Alsace

Almost all the best wines of Alsace are produced from grapes which grow on the east and south facing slopes of the Vosges mountains. The wines are mostly white, dry and very akin to German wines. Unlike other French regions, Alsace wines take their name from the vine producing the grapes and *not* from the village, 'commune' or vineyard. The best known Alsace wines are:

riesling,
sylvaner,
gewürztraminer,
muscat d'Alsace,
tokay d'Alsace.

The label on the Alsace wine bottle shows the name of the grower. Alsace wines are traditionally served in glasses with long stems.

Val de Loire

The wines of the Loire Valley are produced in the famous Châteaux country stretching from Nevers in the centre of France to the Atlantic coast in the west at St-Nazaire. The vineyards are mostly white or rosé with a small number of exceptional sparkling wines. Those red wines which are produced are light. The best known Loire Valley wines are (travelling from east to west):

pouilly fumé,
sancerre,
vouvray*,
saumur*,
rosé d'Anjou,
cabernet d'Anjou,
muscadet.

The best known reds are: chinon and bourgueil.
(* Vouvray and saumur are also sparkling wines.)
As a group of wines, Loire Valley wines are light and are drunk within a short time, 2-3 years only, of their production.

Vins de Provence and the Languedoc

With the extension of the 'appellation contrôlée' system and the development of 'co-opératives' in the wine producing industry, many light table wines, which were formerly simply 'vins de pays' have acquired names by which they are now more commonly known. A vast quantity of undistinguished 'vin ordinaire' of low alcoholic content is still produced in 'le Midi', particularly in the Hérault Department. Among wines of the south, such names are now appearing:

> côtes de Provence,
> costières du Gard,
> côteaux du Languedoc.

Vocabulary

Masculine		Feminine	
client	customer	carte	menu
champagne	champagne	cliente	customer
		commune	'commune'
		co-opérative	co-operative
		marque	make, brand
		montagne	mountain
		vallée	valley

Exercise 24

1 Explain the following terms:
   brut   blanc de blancs   'co-opérative'   grandes marques
   riche (of champagne)   riesling
2 From what district do the following wines come?
   côtes de Provence   Mercier   sylvaner   vouvray   pouilly fumé
   rosé d'Anjou
3 Name five leading champagne firms.
4 Quiz
   Name the champagne produced from white grapes.
   On which town is the Champagne district centred?
   Name a sparkling Loire Valley wine.
   Name a famous rosé of the Loire Valley.
   What district produces a good deal of 'vin ordinaire'?
   Name an Alsace wine.
   Name a red wine from the Loire Valley.
   What does demi-sec imply?
   What sort of wine is pinot noir?
   In what sort of glass do you serve
      champagne,
      Alsace wine?
   What does 'frappé' mean?

What is Moët et Chandon?
What does VDQS stand for? (Check back)
Which is the odd one out:
sancerre, cabernet, sylvaner, saumur
(NB there could be *two* different answers)

Conversation four

Au restaurant
1 Garçon: ...... Et qu'est-ce que vous prenez comme vin, monsieur?
  Client: Vous avez la carte, s'il vous plaît?
  Garçon: Voici, monsieur.
  Client: Voyons, je prendrai une bouteille de muscadet, s'il vous plaît.
  Garçon: Très bien, monsieur.

2 Garçon: ...... Et que voulez-vous comme vin, monsieur? Rouge, blanc, rosé?
  Client: Avez-vous du vin en carafe?
  Garçon: Oui, monsieur.
  Client: Donc, une demi-carafe de rouge, s'il vous plaît.
  Garçon: Bien, monsieur.

3 Garçon: Voulez-vous du vin, monsieur?
  Client: Oui, je prendrai une demi-bouteille de rouge. Non, plutôt, du rosé.
  Garçon: Bien, monsieur. Un rosé d'Anjou?
  Client: Oui, ça va. Et bien frais, s'il vous plaît.
  Garçon: Merci beaucoup.

4 Garçon: Prenez-vous du vin, monsieur?
  Client: Oui. Qu'est-ce que vous avez comme blanc?
  Garçon: Un muscadet, un vin d'Alsace?
  Client: Oui, un vin d'Alsace. Ça va très bien.
  Garçon: Un riesling?
  Client: Oui, c'est ça. Et un peu d'eau fraîche, s'il vous plaît.
  Garçon: Très bien, monsieur.

Language notes

The use of 'du', 'de la', 'de l'' and 'des'

There is no single French word for 'some'. If we wish to say 'some' in French, we have to use one of four words, 'du, de la, de l' or des', depending on the word being considered.

In the various conversations earlier, the expression 'du vin' was used.

Example: Prenez-vous du vin?
         Avez-vous du vin?

We say 'du' in this case because 'vin' is masculine. Other examples are

> du rosé,
> du rouge,

or chosen from previous units:
> du poisson,
> du boeuf,
> du veau.

'Du' then is used with masculine singular words.
 The feminine singular form is 'de la'. Examples of this are:

> de la viande,
> de la sauce,
> de la moutarde.

If the word is singular and beings with a vowel or a silent 'h', 'de l' is used instead of the 'du' or 'de la' form:

> de l'eau (f),
> de l'huile (f),
> de l'ananas (m).

The plural form of 'du, de la and de l'' is 'des'.

> des fraises,
> des légumes,
> des hors-d'oeuvre.

 After an expression of quantity of any sort, the 'du, de la, des' become 'de'.
Hence the expressions which have already been met:

> une bouteille de rosé d'Anjou,
> une demi-bouteille de vin blanc,
> un peu de vin,
> une corbeille de fruits.

De shortens to 'd'' in front of a vowel:
> un peu d'eau fraîche,
> une carafe d'eau fraîche.

Unit 25

Wines of France – Bordeaux region (les vins de Bordeaux)

Aim: To introduce the wines of Bordeaux

The two really great wine producing areas of France are Bordeaux and Burgundy (La Bourgogne).

It is in these two world famous regions that wines of exceptional quality are produced. This does not mean that all the wines coming from these regions are automatically very expensive but many do have an exclusiveness which commands a high price and requires a connoisseur's palate for a true appreciation. In both these regions wines are named after the individual vineyard or property where they are produced and in the Bordeaux region this practice gives rise to the term château bottled or mis en bouteille au château.

Bordeaux

This Unit will be devoted to Bordeaux wines. The bulk of Bordeaux wines are red and red Bordeaux is known in the United Kingdom as a claret. There are six main wine producing areas in the Bordeaux region:

> Médoc,
> Graves,
> St-Emilion,
> Entre-deux-Mers,
> Pomerol,
> Sauternes.

In addition, there are three other regions which are less renowned:

> Côtes de Blaye,
> Côtes de Bourg,
> Côtes de Bordeaux.

Because of the system of 'appellation contrôlée', the term 'bordeaux' is reserved for wines produced in a well defined area on either side of the Gironde estuary and the two large rivers which flow into this estuary, the Garonne and the Dordogne. The whole area is centred on the city of Bordeaux.

Much can be learned from the labels of the wine bottles, which will indicate clearly from which of the districts the wine comes. The term 'bordeaux' or 'bordeaux supérieur' means that the red or white wine is blended from wines of the district and is not exclusive to any one commune or château. Such a wine is obviously cheaper.

The Districts

Médoc

The Médoc is sub-divided into:

> Médoc,
> Haut-Médoc.

Wines from the Haut Médoc are especially highly thought of and of the 28 communes, four are considered exceptional:

> St-Estèphe,
> Pauillac,
> St-Julien,
> Margaux.

The vineyards within each commune are called 'châteaux' and these are graded on a five point scale (grand cru) according to the quality of the wine:

> premier cru,
> deuxième cru,
> troisième cru,
> quatrième cru,
> cinquième cru.

In this way a full pedigree can be given. For example, Château Latour is a 'premier cru' from the commune of Pauillac in the High Médoc of Bordeaux.

Graves

The majority of Graves wines are white. The name 'Graves' appears on the label. Likewise the Graves District is sub-divided into communes, and then by a further sub-division into the vineyards or châteaux.

There is one 'premier grand cru', the 'Château Haut-Brion' from the commune of Pessac. Other red wines of great reputation are:

> Château Latour,
> Château Haut-Bailly.

Among the white wines of Graves are:

> Domaine de Chevalier,
> Château Carbonnieux

St Emilion

The district of St Emilion is on the northern bank of the Dordogne River. According to the classification of 1955 there are three 'crus':

> Premier grand cru classé (a),
> Premier grand cru classé (b),
> Grand cru classé.

Well respected châteaux are:

> Château Ausone,
> Château Cheval-Blanc,
> Château Figeac,
> Clos Fourtet,
> Château Cadet-Bon,
> Château La Tour-Figeac.

Entre-deux-Mers

As its name implies, this region lies between the two great rivers of the region, the Garonne and the Dordogne. The region produces mainly white wines, some of which have acquired 'appellation' standard.

Pomerol

Pomerol, almost entirely surrounded by St Emilion, is the smallest of the wine-producing regions of Bordeaux. The quantities produced are relatively small, so that the prices are comparatively high. Among the premiers grands crus of Pomerol are:

> Château Petrus,
> Château Certan,
> Château Petit-Village.

Sauternes

Although white wines are produced in Graves and Entre-deux-Mers, the bulk of white Bordeaux comes from the last of the six great regions, Sauternes and its neighbour, Barsac. Classifications dates, like Médoc, from 1855 and the most famous communes are:

> Sauternes,
> Bommes,
> Barsac,
> Fargues.

There is one premier grand cru:

> Château d'Yquem (of the Sauternes commune),

a most outstanding white wine, the result of 'pourriture noble' the process of allowing the grapes to rot on the vine to concentrate the sugar content of the grape.

Among the premiers crus of Sauternes are:

Château Latour-Blanche (Bommes commune),
Château Coutet (Barsac),
Château Guiraud (Sauternes commune).

The classification of Sauternes wines extends to 'deuxième cru'.

Vocabulary

Masculine		*Feminine*	
cru	vintage	pourriture	rot

Exercise 25

1 Explain the following terms:
   château   commune   premier cru   deuxième cru
   pourriture noble   1855 classification
2 Name the six great wine-producing districts of Bordeaux.
3 Name four communes in:
   Médoc   Sauternes
4 Associate these wines with their district:
   Château Latour   Château Petrus   Château d'Yquem
   Château Ausone   Domaine de Chevalier
5 Quiz
   What is the Garonne?
   What can you deduce from the term 'bordeaux supérieur'?
   What is Côtes de Blaye?
   When were a) St-Emilion b) Médoc wines classified?
   Which is the smallest of the wine producing regions of Bordeaux?
   On which town is the Bordeaux region centred?
   What is the Dordogne?

Research question

Try to find out from which districts of Bordeaux the following wines come:

Château Margaux,
Château Lascombes,
Château Calon-Ségur,
Château Cadet-Bon,
Château Pape-Clément,
Château Caillon,
Château La Tour-du-Pin-Figeac,
Château Canon,
Château Climens,
Château Montrose.

Give, if possible, the commune and the 'cru'. Find out the current retail price per bottle.

Start a collection of labels from Bordeaux wine bottles for a college compendium.

Unit 26

Wines of France – Burgundy region (les vins de Bourgogne)

Aim: To introduce the wines of Burgundy, Beaujolais and the Rhône Valley

The wine-producing area of Burgundy lies on the west side of the Saône River between Dijon in the north and Mâcon in the south, with the isolated vineyards of Chablis some 120 kms to the north-west of Dijon. Further south from Mâcon, still on the west bank of the Saône, lie the wine-growing districts of Beaujolais, while further south still on either side of the Rhône lie the extensive vineyards of the Côtes du Rhône.

Even greater care in understanding the 'vins de Bourgogne' is needed than for Bordeaux wines. There are five principal areas, six if Beaujolais is included. From north to south, these are:

Chablis,
Côte de Nuits ⎫
Côte de Beaune ⎭ forming the Côte-d'Or,
Côte du Chalonnais,
Côte du Mâconnais,
Beaujolais.

Chablis

Perhaps the finest white wine of all, chablis is sold in four categories:

grand cru chablis,
premier cru chablis,
chablis,
petit chablis.

There are seven grand cru vineyards, of which the most famous are:

Vaudésir,
Les Clos.

However, whatever the 'cru', the name chablis should denote a very acceptable dry white wine.

Côte de Nuits and Côte de Beaune

The wines produced in these two districts are sometimes rather easily confused. Firstly, many vineyards are under multiple ownership and secondly the information on the label needs careful attention to ensure that the contents of the bottle are what is required.

There are three categories in order of quality:

grand cru,
premier cru,
village.

In reverse order, 'village' indicates a wine from any vineyard within the village commune named. Examples of this practice are:

Nuits-St-Georges   (from Côte de Nuits),
Pommard   (from Côte de Beaune),
Volnay   (also from Côte de Beaune).

A 'premier cru' has both the name of the village and the vineyard (climat):

Nuits-St-Georges – Les Vaucrains,
Nuits-St-Georges – Les Cailles.

The 'grands crus' wines have only the name of the vineyard. If in doubt, it is necessary to check if it is the name of the village or the vineyard (climat) which is given on the label. Examples of grands crus are:

Chambertin   (from Gevrey-Chambertin, Côte de Nuits),
Richebourg   (from Vosne-Romanée, Côte de Nuits),
Corton   (Aloxe-Corton, Beaune).

Communes of Nuits and Beaune

Once the principle of naming Burgundy wines has been understood, it is possible to list the villages or communes of the Côte de Nuits and the Côte de Beaune.

The communes of the *Côte de Nuits* are:

Fixin,
Gevrey-Chambertin,
Morey-St-Denis,
Chambolle Musigny,

Vougeot,
Flagey-Echézeaux,
Vosne-Romanée,
Nuits-St-Georges.

The communes of the *Côte de Beaune* are:

Aloxe-Corton,
Pernand-Vergelesses,
Savigny-les-Beaunes,
Beaune,
Pommard,
Volnay,
Meursault,
Chassagne-Montrachet.

Côte du Chalonnais and Côte du Mâconnais

Although wines produced in these areas do not have the reputation of Côte de Nuits and Côte de Beaune, they are widely drunk. Certainly

mâcon rouge,
mâcon blanc and
pouilly-fuissé (a golden mâcon wine),

have an excellent reputation.
'Mâcon village' is a familiar 'appellation' in the United Kingdom.

Beaujolais

Beaujolais wines are produced from the Gamay grape. The area may be divided into three sections, the northernmost area containing the nine great communes of Beaujolais, which are, from north to south:

St Amour,
Juliénas,
Chénas,
Moulin-à-Vent,
Fleurie,
Chiroubles,
Morgon,
Côte de Brouilly,
Brouilly.

Beaujolais wines are classified as

beaujolais grand cru,
beaujolais villages,
beaujolais.

Côtes du Rhône

About 130 communes produce wines under the 'appellation' 'Côtes du Rhône'. 'Côtes du Rhône Village' is reserved for the 16 best communes, some of which are justly famous, mostly from near Avignon:

Tavel,
Gigondas,
Châteauneuf-du-Pape.

as well as the well-known 'Hermitage' wines from a little farther north between Valence and Vienne.

Exercise 26

1 Name the six major wine producing areas of Burgundy.
2 Name two communes in
  Nuits,   Beaune,   Beaujolais.
3 What can be deduced from the following label?

Cuvée des Echevins
MACON LUGNY
Appellation Mâcon Villages Contrôlée
Mise en Bouteille
en France

4 Comment on these three names:
  Clos de Vougeot   Vougeot   Vougeot — Clos de Vougeot
  What part of Burgundy are they from?
5 From what region do these wines come:
  vaudésir   clos blanc de Vougeot   chénas   romanée
  pommard
6 Pair off the following wines with their region of production:
  a) les clos   1 Chablis
  b) juliénas   2 Côte de Nuits
  c) meursault   3 Côte du Mâconnais
  d) pouilly-fuissé   4 Côtes du Rhône
  e) tavel   5 Côte de Beaune
  f) gevrey-chambertin   6 Côte de Beaujolais
7 Quiz
  What is the name of the river which runs through Burgundy?
  Where is Chablis?
  Which town may be said to mark the south extremity of Burgundy?
  What does a) cru b) climat mean?
  Which grape produces beaujolais wine?
  What wine is particularly associated with Tavel?
  What is significant about the term 'village' applied to Côtes du Rhône wines?

Unit 27

The end of the meal (la fin du repas)

Aim: To introduce terms associated with the end of the meal

The meal traditionally ends with coffee, liqueurs and perhaps a small sweet or petits fours.

Section A

Coffee

Other than specialities like café liégeois or Irish coffee, coffee is served as:

> café,
> café crème,
> café filtre.

'Café au lait' is a breakfast drink.

Brandies and liqueurs

A brandy or a liqueur may accompany the coffee. Brandy is served in a 'ballon', as are certain liqueurs. Waisted glasses are commonly used for serving liqueurs.

Brandy

The most widely known brandy is cognac, named after the Cognac district of France in the Charente, to the north of Bordeaux. There are several firms associated with the distillation of cognac and, like whisky, the name of the firm applies to the cognac. These firms are:

> Bisquit,
> Courvoisier,
> Hennessy,
> Hine,
> Martell,
> Otard,
> Rémy Martin.

Cognacs may also be called fine champagne after the part of the Cognac region where the grapes are grown. Cognac is colloquially known as 'une fine'.

Certain initials and star classifications accompany cognacs.

VO	very old,
VSO	very superior old,
VSOP	very superior old pale.

The star system indicates the number of years the cognac has spent in the cask:

***	5 years,
****	6 years,
*****	7 years.

.Other brandies

There are three other less well-known brandies, or more correctly eaux-de-vie, all of which are referred to by their individual names, rather than brandy:

armagnac	from la Gascogne,
calvados	from la Normandie,
marc	a secondary distillation from several fruits or grape.

Café arrosé frequently uses 'marc'.

Alcools blancs

Alcohol can be distilled from various fruits. Collectively these are called 'eaux-de-vie', with the fruit named:

eau-de-vie de poire,
eau-de-vie de fraise.

Framboise, mirabelle, pruneau, quetsch are also used to make 'eaux-de-vie'. Like kirsch, they are frequently used to add distinction to desserts of various sorts, as well as being drunk as a liqueur.

Liqueurs

Liqueurs derive their characteristic flavours from the essences of fruits, plants and herbs in various combinations. The flavours are blended into the alcohol by one of two methods:

infusion,
percolation.

The resulting spirit is distilled to increase its alcoholic content and intensify the predominant flavour. The spirits are finally sweetened.

Liqueurs may have quite a distinctive fruit taste of, for example, banana, peach, plum or pear. They are not 'eaux-de-vie', which are usually colourless: liqueurs are coloured, generally artifcially, at some point in the process of their manufacture. Other liqueurs are known by name. These include:

Liqueur		Taste
Chartreuse	Chartreuse verte (stronger)	secret formula of herbs
	Chartreuse jaune	
Bénédictine DOM		secret formula
B et B		brandy and benedictine
izarra verte		herbs
jaune		
Cointreau		orange
Grand Marnier		orange
Triple Sec (curaçao)		orange
crème de menthe		mint
crème de cassis		blackcurrant
crème de cacao		chocolate
cherry heering		cherry
Vieille Cure		brandy type
Verveine du Velay		herbs
Tia Maria		coffee

Friandises

Various friandises may accompany coffee served at the end of the meal. Besides a selection of chocolates, the more common are:

> petits fours (secs),
> truffes au chocolat,
> petits fours aux amandes,
> fruits confits,
> marrons glacés,
> dragées.

Section B Eaux minérales

No course would be complete without mention of natural or spring waters. These bottled waters are favoured by some people for non-alcoholic, medicinal or diuretic purposes. Each has its own property and taste and is declared to be of 'intérêt public'.

The most widespread are:

> Eau de Vichy,
> Perrier (gazeuse),
> Volvic,
> Contrexéville,
> Évian,
> Vittel,
> Vitteloise,
> Badoit.

Exercise 27

1 What are the following?
  ballon   une fine   calvados   eau-de-vie   curaçao
2 What is the difference between green and yellow Chartreuse?
  To what other liqueur does this apply?
3 State whether the following are brandy, liqueur or eau-de-vie:
  kirsch   Triple Sec   Verveine du Velay   calvados   Hine
4 Name five firms distilling brandy.
5 Name five 'eaux de source'.
6 Which liqueur do you associate with?
  mint   a mixture of liqueur and brandy   chocolate   coffee
  orange flavour
7 What are the following?
  Courvoisier   armagnac   Vittel   izarra   Perrier
8 What is the significance of the following?
  VSOP   *****   café au lait   marc   fine champagne

Preparation

Produce a map of France showing the area or town from which the following wines, eaux-de-vie, liqueurs or distinctive terms come:

calvados   niçoise   Vittel   Bayonne   Vichy   Chartreuse
Périgueux   brie   dieppoise   Velay   provençale   chablis
Savoie   mâcon blanc   châteauneuf-du-pape   cognac
champagne   roquefort   rosé d'Anjou   lyonnaise

What do you associate with each term?

Revision test 5 (Units 22 – 26)

1 Terms

  a) Explain the following terms:
     appellation contrôlée   vin mousseux   une carafe
     vin de pays   château
  b) Give five principal wine-producing regions of France.
  c) Explain the following:
     flûte   mis en bouteille   pétillant   sec   Côtes du Rhône
  d) Where are the following grapes principally used?
     pinot noir   gamay   cabernet sauvignon   traminer
     chardonnay

2 Terms

a) Explain the following terms:
   brut   blanc de blancs   Moët et Chandon   riesling
   muscadet

3 Wines of Bordeaux and Burgundy

a) Give five of the main wine-producing areas of Bordeaux.
b) Associate the following wines with their district:
   Château Latour   Barsac   Château Haut Brion
   Château d'Yquem   Entre-deux-Mers
c) From which area of Burgundy do the following wines come?
   nuits-St-Georges   chablis   chambertin   volnay   juliénas
d) Pair off the following wines with their area of production:
   châteauneuf-du-pape   Beaujolais
   vougeot   Côte du Mâconnais
   pouilly-fuissé   Côtes du Rhône
   pommard   Côte de Nuits
   moulin-à-vent   Côte de Beaune

4 Brandies and liqueurs

a) Explain these terms:
   VSOP   Martell   calvados   eau-de-vie   *****
b) Give the names of five firms retailing cognac.
c) Comment on the following:
   Cointreau   B et B   crème de menthe   Perrier   Evian

Aural comprehension 5

Listen carefully to the snatches of conversation read to you. Each conversation will be read twice. After each conversation, answer the question, a), b), c) or d), according to which answer you think is the best.

1 Did the man order a wine from?
   a) Burgundy
   b) Alsace
   c) Loire Valley
   d) Bordeaux

2 Did the customer want?
   a) a vin de pays
   b) a full bottle
   c) a wine by the carafe
   d) a glass of wine

3 What wine was required?
   a) a rosé
   b) a white
   c) a sparkling wine
   d) a red

4 What wine was ordered?
   a) a sweet wine
   b) a dry white wine
   c) a sparkling wine
   d) a light red wine

5 Where did the wine come from?
   a) Alsace
   b) Champagne
   c) Bourgogne
   d) Provence

6 Was the order for a wine from?
   a) Alsace
   b) Bordeaux
   c) Loire Valley
   d) Champagne

7 What was the enquiry about?
   a) red wine
   b) a champagne
   c) a cognac
   d) a mineral water
9 Was the wine ordered?
   a) a rosé
   b) a sauternes
   c) a claret
   d) a sparkling wine

8 Was the order for?
   a) a liqueur
   b) a coffee
   c) a cognac
   d) an 'eau-de-vie'
10 Would you expect the answer to be?
   a) châteauneuf-du-pape
   b) mâcon rouge
   c) chablis
   d) nuits-St-Georges

Supplementary test paper 1

1 Explain: à la carte, buffet froid, julienne, carbon(n)ade, consommé, Du Barry, Vichy, maison, entrecôte, à l'anglaise.

2 *Meats*   Give the English for the following cuts: côtelette, escalope, blanquette, aloyau, tête, filet, gigot, selle.
   Give the English for the following preparations: paupiette, ragoût, braisé, pané, bien cuit, saignant, rôti.

3 *Fish*   Give the English for: merlan, cabillaud, saumon, plie, raie, hareng.
   Explain: goujon, darne, suprême, meunière.
   What fish do you associate with: en colère, Véronique, aux amandes, au beurre noir, au bleu.

4 Match up: a) olives   1 à l'huile
              b) sardines   2 maison
              c) huîtres   3 aux pommes
              d) jambon   4 au gratin
              e) pâté   5 farcies
              f) tomates   6 noires
              g) tarte   7 à l'orange
              h) chou-fleur   8 la douzaine
              i) melon   9 de Paris
              j) sorbet   10 au porto

5 Explain: bisque, velouté, glace, barquette, brunoise, fumé.
6 Complete: ———— vertes   sole ————
              ———— Anna   saucisson ————
              ———— d'agneau   purée ————
              ———— farcis   tournedos ————
              ———— Crécy   poulet ————

7 To what could the following terms apply?
macédoine, corbeille, flambés, camembert, Condé, Belle-Hélène, mousse, quiche, Mornay, au jus.

8 More difficult pairs:

a)	fonds	1	au beurre
b)	céleri	2	à la neige
c)	asperges	3	d'artichaut
d)	oignons	4	en cocotte
e)	pommes	5	à la noix
f)	oeufs	6	braisé
g)	omelette	7	braisés
h)	gîte	8	au poivre
i)	rôti	9	de porc
j)	steak	10	nature

10 Explain:
claret, Burgundy, brie, viennoise, minute, Parmentier, chambré, kirsch, bombe, frappé.

Supplementary test paper 2

1 Explain: table d'hôte, entrée, potage, plat du jour, couvert, coupe, bain-marie, terrine, crudités, escargots.

2 What are these methods of service or preparation in English? Give an explanation if more appropriate.
frappé, râpé, fricassé, sauté, varié, haché, pané, sucré, praliné, rafraîchi.

3 What would you have:
à l'anglaise, à la neige, à l'orange, au poivre, au beurre noir, à l'ail, à la confiture, au citron, au vin blanc, à la fraise?

4 Which vegetable do you associate with:
flamande, portugaise, Du Barry, Doria, Crécy, Clamart?

5 Pair off:

a)	épinards	1	Mornay
b)	maïs	2	verte
c)	sauce	3	pilaf
d)	tournedos	4	Rossini
e)	salade	5	de veau
f)	pommes	6	en branches
g)	omelette	7	Washington
h)	riz	8	de table
i)	cuisseau	9	d'agneau
j)	selle	10	au fromage

6 Explain:
vol-au-vent, choucroute, flûte, au gratin, rognons, volaille, fondue, ballottines, en croûte.

7 Is A or B correct?

		A	*B*
1	pommes	persillées	sautés
2	aubergines	farcies	farcis
3	filet de plie	frite	grillé
4	plateau	de fromages	de choix
5	vacherin	à la fraise	aux fraises
6	macédoine de	crème	fruits
7	tarte	à la pomme	aux pommes
8	carottes	râpées	râpés
9	banane	flambée	flambé
10	pommes	paille	pailles

8 Pair off:

a)	filet de sole	1	à la noix
b)	poulet	2	niçoise
c)	gîte	3	de veau
d)	salade	4	chasseur
e)	au beurre	5	farcies
f)	tomates	6	de pomme
g)	escalope	7	Véronique
h)	oignons	8	fumée
i)	beignet	9	braisés
j)	truite	10	noir

9 Complete, with an appropriate term, correctly spelt:

ananas ———— corbeille de ———— compote de ————

profiteroles au ———— riz ———— ———— farcis

———— verts ———— grillée ———— noires

———— Condé

10 What are the following in English? Explain if more appropriate.
batterie de cuisine, sommelier, garçon, pâtisserie, chinois, dariole, Chantilly, bouquet garni, croûtons, bouillon.

Supplementary test paper 3

1 Supply the word that fills the gap:
tarte ...... pommes, pommes ...... anglaise, ragoût ...... boeuf, sole ...... -femme, caneton ...... orange, oeufs ...... mayonnaise, oeufs ...... cocotte, éclair ...... chocolat, pommes ...... neige, truite ...... bleu

2 Explain the following terms:
chausson, beignet, bombe, couvert, croissant, corbeille, plateau, fricassé, carafe, cognac.

111

3 What vegetables do you associate with:
florentine, Du Barry, Clamart, Doria, Parmentier?
What method of preparation is indicated by:
niçoise, indienne, julienne, brunoise, mirepoix?

4 Complete the following pairs:

a) haricots	1 au gratin
b) carottes	2 paille
c) choux	3 sautées
d) petits	4 d'artichauts
e) courgettes	5 verts
f) fonds	6 belges
g) pointes	7 râpées
h) endives	8 de Bruxelles
i) pommes	9 pois
j) chou-fleur	10 d'asperges

With which vegetable would the following preparation be associated?

Vichy   à l'anglaise   braisées   en robe de chambre
sauce Mornay

5 Which is the correct spelling, A or B?

	A	B
côtelette de porc	grillé	grillée
gigot d'agneau	rôti	rôtie
carré d'agneau	persillé	persillée
boeuf	braisé	braisée
escalope de veau	pané	panée

6 *Desserts*   Explain: sorbet, crêpe, mousse, Condé, coupe, barquette, macédoine, pâtisserie, savarin

7 Give the English for these fruits:
citron, framboise, abricot, poire, fraise, pamplemousse, pêche, raisin, mirabelle, ananas.

8 Which fruit would accompany or be associated with:
au kirsch, flambées, au vin rouge, au porto, jus, rafraîchi, Belle-Hélène, compote?

9 Explain:
à la carte, champagne, Burgundy, claret, service non compris, appellation contrôlée, sec/brut, praliné, espagnole, Béchamel.

Multiple choice exercises

The following three multiple choice exercises may be used as test papers for students who have studied the wine industry of France or as research exercises for those who have as yet no detailed knowledge of the topic.

Multiple choice exercise 1 – Wine industry 1

1 Wines of Alsace are named after
 a) the region.
 b) the village.
 c) the vine.
 d) rivers.

2 Alsace wines are traditionally drunk in a
 a) ballon.
 b) flûte.
 c) coupe.
 d) verre à pied.

3 Alsace wines are produced on the Eastern slopes of
 a) Vosges.
 b) Jura.
 c) Ardennes.
 d) Black Forest.

4 Alsace wines are most akin to
 a) champagne.
 b) German hock.
 c) white burgundies.
 d) clarets.

5 The champagne industry is centred on the town of
 a) Metz.
 b) Reims.
 c) Nancy.
 d) Strasbourg.

6 Champagne is mostly made from
 a) white grapes.
 b) black grapes.
 c) black and white grapes.
 d) Gamay grapes.

7 Champagne should be drunk in a
 a) flûte.
 b) verre à pied.
 c) ballon.
 d) coupe.

8 Which is the odd one out?
 a) Krug
 b) Chambéry
 c) Veuve Clicquot
 d) Mercier

9 The Loire Valley produces predominantly
 a) white wines.
 b) rosé wines.
 c) red wines.
 d) sparkling wines.

10 Anjou is well-known for its
   a) rosé.
   b) sparkling wines.
   c) red.
   d) white.

11 Muscadet is
   a) a Loire Valley wine.
   b) a burgundy.
   c) a claret.
   d) a vin ordinaire.

12 Chinon and bourgueil are exceptional because
   a) they are sparkling.
   b) they are red.
   c) they are 'appellation contrôlée'.
   d) they are served chilled.

13 Sancerre and pouilly are
   a) red burgundies.
   b) Côte de Beaune wines.
   c) Loire Valley wines.
   d) Bordeaux wines.

14 Chablis is best served
   a) chambré.
   b) chilled although red.
   c) chilled.
   d) with ice.

15 The most northerly of the Burgundian wine-producing regions are found in
   a) Côtes du Nord.
   b) Côte de Nuits.
   c) Côte du Mâconnais.
   d) Côte de Beaune.

16 The term 'côte' refers to
   a) a hillside.
   b) a vineyard.
   c) a vintage.
   d) a co-operative.

17 Côte de Nuits and Côte de Beaune are
   a) Bordeaux wines.
   b) Mâcon wines.
   c) Burgundy wines.
   d) Rhône Valley wines.

18 Beaujolais is
   a) south of Mâcon.
   b) part of Mâcon.
   c) north of the Côte de Beaune.
   d) part of the Rhône Valley system.

19 Moulin-à-vent, fleurie, chénas and juliénas are all wines from
  a)   Burgundy.
  b)   Bordeaux.
  c)   Beaujolais.
  d)   Côtes du Rhône.
20 The wine associated with Avignon is
  a)   vouvray.
  b)   aloxe-corton.
  c)   châteauneuf-du-pape.
  d)   moselle.

Multiple choice exercise 2 – Wine industry 2

1 What have the following wines in common – vouvray, muscadet, sancerre?
  a)   burgundies
  b)   clarets
  c)   champagnes
  d)   Loire Valley wines
2 In Burgundy the term 'grand cru' refers to
  a)   the vineyard.
  b)   the commune.
  c)   the village.
  d)   the year of production.
3 The Hospices de Beaune are famous for
  a)   vineyards.
  b)   bottling processes.
  c)   cellars.
  d)   auctions.
4 Where are the following wines from – meursault, pommard, volnay?
  a)   Côte de Beaune
  b)   Chablis
  c)   Bordeaux
  d)   Mâcon
5 Entre-deux-Mers is
  a)   claret.
  b)   Côtes de Rhône.
  c)   white.
  d)   sparkling.
6 Sauternes is
  a)   white.
  b)   red.
  c)   dry.
  d)   rosé.
7 Most Médoc wines are
  a)   white.
  b)   red.
  c)   sparkling.
  d)   rosé.

8 St-Estèphe, Margaux, Pauillac are communes of
  a) St-Emilion.
  b) Sauternes.
  c) Graves.
  d) Médoc.

9 The term 'Bordeaux' means
  a) a high quality wine.
  b) a claret.
  c) a blended wine.
  d) a white wine.

10 In Bordeaux the term 'cru' as in 'premier cru' refers to
  a) the vineyard.
  b) the classification of the wine.
  c) the château.
  d) the vintage year.

11 St-Emilion is
  a) a bordeaux.
  b) a graves.
  c) a sauternes.
  d) a pomerol.

12 Sauternes, barsac and bommes are all
  a) white.
  b) red.
  c) rosé.
  d) sparkling.

13 A good deal of 'vin ordinaire' is produced in
  a) Gard.
  b) Var.
  c) Ariège.
  d) Hérault.

14 Côtes de Blaye and Côtes de Bourg are lesser known wines from
  a) Burgundy.
  b) Côtes du Rhône.
  c) Bordeaux.
  d) Alsace.

15 In Bordeaux 'château' refers to
  a) the vintage.
  b) the vineyard.
  c) the producer.
  d) the district.

16 Château d'Yquem is the only 'premier grand cru' from
  a) Médoc.
  b) Graves.
  c) Barsac.
  d) Sauternes.

17 Appellation contrôlée ensures that
   a) the quality is good.
   b) the alcoholic content is guaranteed.
   c) the wine comes from the region stated.
   d) the wine is less than 11°.

18 Anjou refers to a wine from
   a) Alsace.
   b) Loire Valley.
   c) Rhône Valley.
   d) Burgundy.

19 Côtes de Provence refers to wine produced in
   a) Bordeaux.
   b) Provence.
   c) Côtes du Rhône.
   d) Languedoc.

20 In Burgundy the name 'Chambertin' refers to
   a) a producer.
   b) a village.
   c) a vineyard.
   d) a commune.

Multiple choice exercise 3 – Wine industry 3

1 Where do the following wines come from – riesling and sylvaner?
   a) Moselle
   b) Alsace
   c) Loire Valley
   d) Chablis

2 Burgundian wines are named after
   a) the vine.
   b) the grape.
   c) the commune.
   d) the producer.

3 Aloxe-Corton is produced in
   a) Côte de Nuits.
   b) Côtes du Rhône.
   c) Côte du Mâconnais.
   d) Côte de Beaune.

4 What type of wine is vouvray?
   a) sparkling.
   b) hock.
   c) claret.
   d) burgundy.

5 White wines of the Loire include
   a) graves.
   b) mâcon.
   c) sauternes.
   d) sancerre.

6 A commune of the Médoc is

   a) Barsac.

   b) St-Estèphe.

   c) Brouilly.

   d) Braye.

7 White wines of the Loire Valley include

   a) graves.

   b) pouilly-fuissé.

   c) muscadet.

   d) moulin-à-vent.

8 Bordeaux classification dates from

   a) 1855.

   b) 1914.

   c) 1930.

   d) 1945.

9 'Pourriture noble' is a process in producing

   a) bordeaux.

   b) claret.

   c) sauternes.

   d) barsac.

10 'Appellation contrôlée' refers to

   a) the district.

   b) the vineyard.

   c) the producer.

   d) the blend of wine.

11 The bulk of 'vin ordinaire' is produced in

   a) Bordeaux.

   b) Languedoc.

   c) Provence.

   d) Burgundy.

12 What type of wine is tavel?

   a) côtes du Rhône

   b) côtes de Provence

   c) imported

   d) vin ordinaire

13 In Burgundy the term 'village' indicates wine from a specific

   a) vineyard.

   b) producer.

   c) blend.

   d) a grand cru.

14 Nuits-St-Georges is a

   a) commune.

   b) vineyard.

   c) 'domain'.

   d) region.

15 Côte d'Or is a
  a) commune.
  b) department.
  c) village.
  d) wine.
16 Two important wine-producing departments are
  a) Saône-et-Loire and Rhône.
  b) Garonne and Cognac.
  c) Moselle and Loire.
  d) Gironde and Cognac.
17 Mâcon wine is
  a) red.
  b) white.
  c) white and red.
  d) rosé.
18 What type of wine is entre-deux-mers?
  a) claret
  b) white bordeaux
  c) white burgundy
  d) Loire Valley
19 Which is the beaujolais?
  a) cabernet
  b) brouilly
  c) hermitage
  d) gewürztraminer
20 Pomerol and St-Emilion are
  a) communes in Burgundy.
  b) communes in Beaujolais.
  c) areas in Côtes de Provence.
  d) Bordeaux districts.

Reading items for aural comprehension exercises

Aural comprehension 1

Read the following words *twice* each to the class. After each word allow a few seconds for the students to decide which of the preparations suggested at the end of Unit 7 best accompanies the vegetable.

1 asperges	**6** tomates
2 haricots verts	**7** chou-fleur
3 petits pois	**8** macédoine
4 champignons	**9** fèves
5 endives	**10** épinards

Aural comprehension 2

Read the following ten sentences *twice* each. After each sentence allow the students a few moments to answer the questions set out for this test at the end of Unit 11.

1 Que voulez-vous comme légumes, monsieur?
2 Voulez-vous le poisson, monsieur?
3 Je prendrai la salade russe.
4 Je prendrai une côtelette de porc grillée.
5 Je prendrai les carottes Vichy.
6 Voulez-vous les paupiettes de sole, madame?
7 Que voulez-vous comme viande, monsieur? Le steak, le veau ou le porc?
   Je prendrai le filet de boeuf, s'il vous plaît.
8 Bien, monsieur, le steak. Et avec ça?
   Les pommes chips, s'il vous plaît.
9 Bien, monsieur, le steak. Comment le voulez-vous?
   A point, s'il vous plaît.
10 Et que voulez-vous comme poisson, madame?
   Je prendrai la truite.
   Et comment la voulez-vous?
   Aux amandes, s'il vous plaît.

Aural comprehension 3

Read the following short snatches of conversation *twice* in all. After reading each conversation allow the students a few seconds in which to study the suggested answers set out at the end of Unit 17 and choose which one they think most appropriate.

1 Voulez-vous les tomates, les carottes ou les olives?
2 Avez-vous choisi le cabillaud ou la truite?
3 Deux crèmes Crécy, s'il vous plaît.
4 Voulez-vous le porc, le boeuf ou le poulet?
   Non, merci. Je prendrai l'agneau.
5 Voulez-vous le porc, le boeuf ou l'agneau?
   Pour moi, le gigot.
6 Et qu'est-ce que vous prenez après?
7 Voulez-vous une glace, un fruit ou une crêpe?
   Je prendrai des cerises, s'il vous plaît.
8 Prenez-vous la tarte aux pommes, aux pruneaux, à l'abricot ou à l'orange?
   Pour moi, la tarte aux pruneaux.
9 Que voulez-vous après, monsieur, une glace, un fruit ou un fromage?
   Je prendrai du camembert, s'il vous plaît.
10 Que voulez-vous comme fromage, monsieur?
   Du roquefort, s'il vous plaît.

Aural comprehension 4

Read the following ten items to the group, repeating each item once. After each item allow a few seconds for the students to answer the questions set out at the end of Unit 20.

1 filet de boeuf grillé
2 sauce lyonnaise
3 sauce Réforme
4 sauce bigarade
5 sauce Robert
6 sauce madère
7 poulet sauté
8 sole Véronique
9 champagne
10 panaché

Aural comprehension 5

Read the following short snatches of conversation *twice*. After each conversation allow the students a few seconds in which to study the suggested answers set out at the end of Unit 27.

1 Que voulez-vous comme vin, monsieur?
   Je prendrai un rosé d'Anjou.
2 Voulez-vous une demi-bouteille ou une bouteille?
   Avez-vous du vin en carafe?
3 Avez-vous du sauternes?
4 Avez-vous du chablis?
5 Je prendrai une bouteille de riesling, s'il vous plaît.
6 Voulez-vous le Moët et Chandon ou le Veuve Clicquot?
7 Prenez-vous une bouteille de Perrier?
8 Je prendrai du Cointreau.
9 Avez-vous du blanc? Bien, je prendrai le barsac.
10 Que prenez-vous avec les huîtres?

Glossary
French – English

Abbreviations

adj	adjective
f	feminine
It	Italian
lit	literal translation
m	masculine
pl	plural
ct	culinary term
tt	technical term

ct   culinary term   This indicates that the French word is used to describe a process or method of preparation or that it may be a dedication.

tt   technical term   This indicates that the French term is used in English as there is no acceptable translation.

In both cases the number indicates the unit in which the term is introduced.

French		English
à		to, at, in
abats les (m)		offal
aboyeur (m)		barker
abricot (m)		apricot
agneau (m)		lamb
Agnès-Sorel (velouté)	ct4	Agnès-Sorel
aiglefin (m)*		haddock
ail (m)		garlic
alcool (m)		alcohol
Alexandra	ct15	Alexandra
allumette (f)	ct8	'matchstick'
Aloxe-Corton		a Côte de Beaune commune; a wine
aloyau (m)		sirloin
Alsace		region of France
alsacienne	ct7	Alsatian; in the style of Alsace
amande (f)		almond
armoricaine	ct19	Armoricaine; in the Breton style
ananas (m)		pineapple
anchois (m)		anchovy
andouille (de Vire) (f)	ct3	'andouille';
andouillette (f)		small 'andouille', chitterling
anglaise (adj)	ct5	English style

* There are several acceptable alternative spellings, including aigrefin, églefin.

  Haddock is used for smoked haddock.

anguille (f)		eel
Anna	ct8	Anna
appellation contrôlée	tt23	appellation contrôlée
apprenti (m)		apprentice
après		after
arachide (f)		groundnut
armagnac (m)	tt27	Armagnac; a brandy
arrosé (adj)		lengthened with wine
artichaut (m)		artichoke
asperge (f)		asparagus
aspic (m)		aspic
assiette (f)		plate
au, à la, aux		with, to, at
Aurore	ct18	Aurore
Ausone (Château)		a St-Emilion wine
avec		with
avez-vous?		have you?
Avignon		Avignon — a town in southern France
avocat (m)		avocado
baba (m)	tt17	baba (rum)
bain-marie (m)	tt22	bain-marie
banane (f)		banana
ballon (m)		'ballon', brandy glass
ballottine (f)	tt13	ballottine
bande (f)		pastry base, slice
barquette (f)	tt15	barquette, pastry case
Barsac		region of Bordeaux
barsac (m)		the wine of that region
basilic (m)		basil
batterie (f)		kitchen equipment
bavarois (m) bavaroise (f)	tt15	Bavarian cream, bavarois
Bayonne		town in the south-west of France
béarnaise	ct18	béarnaise; in the style of Béarn
Beaujolais (m)		wine-producing district
beaujolais (m)		wine from Beaujolais
Beaune		town in Burgundy
beaune (m)		wine from Beaune
Beaune, Côte de		wine-producing district
bécasse (f)		woodcock
béchamel	tt18	béchamel (sauce)
beignet (m)		fritter, doughnut
belge (adj)		Belgian
Belle-Hélène	tt&ct15	Belle-Hélène
Bénédictine (f)		Benedictine liqueur
B et B		brandy and benedictine

Bercy	ct18	Bercy; a region of France
betterave (f)		beetroot
beurre (m)		butter
beurre maître d'hôtel	tt19	maître d'hôtel butter
beurre manié	tt18	beurre manié
beurre noir	tt19	beurre noir
beurre noisette	tt19	beurre noisette
bien		good, well
biftek (m)		steak
bigarade (f)		bitter orange
bisque (f)	tt4	bisque
Bisquit		a brandy
blanc, blanche (adj)		white
blanchaille (f)		whitebait
blanquette (f)	tt11	blanquette, a white stew
Blaye, Côtes de Blaye		a wine district in the Bordeaux region
bleu (adj)		blue
au bleu	tt6&10	au bleu
bleu d'Auvergne (m)		a cheese
bleu de Bresse		a cheese
blond (adj)		blond, pale (roux)
boeuf (m)		beef
boisson (f)		drink
bol (m)		bowl
bolonaise	ct9	bolonaise, in the style of Bologna
bombe (f)	tt16	bombe
bommes (m)		a Sauternes wine; a commune.
bonne-femme	ct15	bonne-femme
bonne-maman	ct12	bonne-maman
bonjour		good morning
Bordeaux		town in south-west France
bordeaux (m)		wine from Bordeaux
bordelaise	ct10	bordelaise; in the Bordeaux style
bouchée (f)		
bouchée à la reine	tt11	large vol-au-vent
boudin (m)		black pudding
bouillabaisse (f)	tt6	bouillabaisse
bouilli (adj)		boiled
bouillon (m)	tt4	bouillon, stock
boulangère	ct19	boulangère; lit. in the style of the baker's wife
bouquet (m)		bouquet, aroma; prawn
bouquet garni	tt21	bouquet garni
Bourg, Côtes de		a Bordeaux wine-producing district
Bourgogne (f)		Burgundy

bourguignon -ne (adj)	ct10	bourguignon; in the Burgundian style
bourgueil (m)		a Loire Valley wine
Boursin (m)		a cheese
bouteille (f)		bottle
branche (f)		leaf, lit. branch
Bresse	ct13	Bresse; a town in Burgundy
breton -ne (adj)	ct7	Breton; in Breton style
brie (m)		a cheese
brigade (f)		team (in the kitchen)
brioche (f)	tt8	brioche
brochet (m)		pike
broche (f)		spit
brochette (f)		small spit, skewer
brouillé (adj)		scrambled
brouilly (m)		a Beaujolais wine
brun -e (adj)		brown
brunoise	tt7	brunoise
brut (adj)		very dry (champagne)
bruxelloise	ct19	bruxelloise; in the style of Brussels
bûche (f) de Noël		Yule log
buffet (m)	tt1	buffet
buffet froid		cold buffet
ça		that
ça va		all right
cabernet d'Anjou (m)		a Loire Valley wine
Cabernet Sauvignon		a variety of grape
cabillaud (m)		fresh cod
cacao (m)		cocoa
Cadet-Bon (Château)		a St-Emilion wine
café (m)		coffee
café au lait		(breakfast) coffee with milk
café crème		coffee with cream or milk
caille (f)		quail
Cailles Les		a Nuits-St-Georges wine
calvados (m)	tt27	calvados, an eau-de-vie
camembert (m)		a cheese
camomille (f)		camomile
campagne (f)		countryside
canard (m)		duck
canard sauvage		wild duck
caneton (m)		duckling
cannelle (f)		cinnamon
canneloni (It)		a pasta
cantal (m)		a cheese

câpre (f)		caper
carafe (f)	tt23	carafe
caramel (m)		caramel
carbon(n)ade (f)	tt10	carbon(n)ade
Carbonnieux (Château)		a Graves wine
cardinal	ct18	cardinal
carotte (f)		carrot
carré (m) (d'agneau)		best end
carré de l'est (m)		a cheese
carte (f)		menu
à la carte	tt1	à la carte
casserole (f)		saucepan
cassoulet (m)	tt7	cassoulet
cassis (m)		blackcurrant
caviar (m)		caviar
Cayenne, poivre de		Cayenne pepper
céleri (m)		celery
cerfeuil (m)		chervil
cèpe, ceps (m)		variety of mushroom
cerise (f)		cherry
Certan (Château)		a Pomerol wine
cervelle (f)		brains
c'est		it is
Chablis		a region north-west of Dijon
chambertin (m)		a Côte de Nuits wine
Chambolle-Musigny (m)		a Côte de Nuits wine; a commune
Chambourcy		a make of yoghurt
chambré		at room temperature
Champagne (f)		the champagne producing district
champagne (m)		champagne
fine champagne (f)		a brandy
champignon (m)		mushroom
Chantilly (crème)	ct17	Chantilly
chapelure (f)		breadcrumbs
chapon (m)		capon
Charente (f)		a district in West France
charcuterie (f)		pork meats
Chardonnay		a variety of grape
Charles Heidsieck		a champagne
charlotte (f)	tt15	charlotte
Chartreuse (f) jaune verte		a liqueur
Chassagne-Montrachet (m)		a Beaune wine; a commune
chasseur (m)	ct10	chasseur; lit. huntsman
château (m)		castle, estate, country-house

chateaubriand (m)	tt10	a steak
châteauneuf-du-pape (m)		a Côtes du Rhône wine
chaud -e (adj)		warm, hot
chaud-froid (m)	tt13	chaud-froid
chausson (m)		turnover
chef (m)		chef
chénas (m)		a Beaujolais wine
Chenin blanc		a variety of grape
cherry heering (m)		a liqueur
Chevalier, Domaine de		a Graves wine
chèvre (f)		goat
chevreuil (m)		roebuck,
chinon (m)		a Loire Valley wine
chinois (m)		conical strainer, chinois
chip (m)		crisp, game chip
chiroubles (m)		a Beaujolais wine
chocolat (m)		chocolate
choisi		chosen
avez-vous choisi?		have you chosen?
choix (m)		choice
chou (m)		cabbage
choucroute (f)		sauerkraut
chou de Bruxelles (m)		Brussels sprout
chou-fleur (m)		cauliflower
ciboulette (f)		chive
cinquième		fifth
ciseaux (m)		scissors
citron (m)		lemon
civet (m)		jugged hare
clair-e (adj)		clear
Clamart	ct11	Clamart
client(e) (m & f)		customer
clos (m)		vineyard, domain, estate
Les Clos		a Chablis wine
clou de girofle (m)		clove
clouté (adj)		studded
cocotte (f)	tt9	cocotte, small dish
coeur (m)		heart
Cognac		a district in western France
cognac (m)		brandy, cognac
Cointreau (m)		a liqueur
colère, en	ct6	en colère; lit. in anger
colin (m)		hake
comme		as, like
commis (m)		assistant chef
commune (f)	tt25	smallest administrative district in France; sub-division of a 'département'

compote (f)		stewed fruit
compris (adj)		included
non compris		not included
comté (m)		a cheese
concassé (adj)	tt20	concassé, concassed
concombre (m)		cucumber
Condé	ct15	Condé
confit (m)		preserve
confit (adj)		conserved
confiture (f)		jam
congélateur (m)		deep-freeze, freezer
conseil (m)		advice
consommé (m)	tt4	consommé, clear soup
continental -e (adj)	ct11	continental
contre-filet (m)		sirloin of beef
Contrexéville		a bottled water
co-opérative (f)		a wine co-operative
coq (m)		chicken, cockerel
coque (f)		cockle
à la coque (oeuf)		soft boiled
coquillage (m)		shellfish
corbeille (f)		basket
cornet (m)		horn
cornichon (m)		gherkin
corton		a Beaune wine
côte (f)		hillside; flank (animal)
côtelette (f)		chop, cutlet
côte de Brouilly		a Beaujolais wine
Côte-d'Or (f)		a French department in Burgundy
coulommiers (m)		a cheese
coupe (f)	tt15	cup; coupe
Courvoisier		a brandy
courgette (f)		marrow, courgette
court-bouillon (m)	tt19	stock, court-bouillon
couteau (m)		knife
Coutet (Château)		a Sauternes wine
couvert (m)		cover, cover charge
crabe (m)		crab
Crécy	ct4	Crécy
crème (f)		cream
crème de cacao		a liqueur
crème de menthe		a liqueur
créole (adj)	ct15	créole; in Créole style
crêpe (f)	tt16	crêpe, pancake
cresson (m)		watercress
cressonnière	ct4	cressonnière

crevette (f) rose		shrimp
croque-monsieur (m)	tt14	croque-monsieur
croquette (f)	tt8	croquette
croûte (f)		crust, pastry
en croûte		in pastry
croûte-au-pot	ct4	croûte-au-pot
croûton (m)	tt19	croûton
cru-e (adj)		raw, uncooked
cru (m)		growth
crudités (f)		raw vegetable salad
creux -se (adj)		hollow
cuillère (f) cuiller (f)		spoon
cuisine (f)		kitchen; art of cooking
cuisinière (f)		cooker, stove
cuisseau (m)		leg of veal or pork
cuissot (m)		leg of large game
cuit-e (adj)		cooked
culotte (f)		rump
curaçao (m)		a liqueur
cuvée (f)		vat; contents of the vat
Danone		make of yoghurt
darne (f)		cutlet (of fish)
datte (f)		date
daube (f)		meat stew
en daube	tt10	en daube
dauphine	ct8	dauphine; lit. in the style of the Dauphin's wife
daurade (f)		sea bream
de, du, de la, des		of
délice (m)		fillet of fish
demi-		half
demi-bouteille (f)		half-bottle
demi-douzaine (f)		half a dozen
demi-sel (m)		a cheese
département (m)		the French equivalent of an English county; department
dessert (m)		dessert
deux		two
deuxième (adj)		second
diable	ct13	diable; devilled
dieppoise	ct6	dieppoise; in the Dieppe style
Dijon		the main town in Côte-d'Or
dinde (f)		turkey
dindon (m)		turkey
dindonneau (m)		young turkey
domaine (m)		domain, estate

donc		so, therefore
dorade (f)		an alternative spelling of daurade, though widely used
Dordogne (f)		district in central southern France
Doria	ct19	Doria
doux -ce (adj)		sweet, mild
douzaine (f)		dozen
dragée (f)		sugared almond
du, de la, des		some; of the
Du Barry	ct4	Du Barry
duchesse	ct8	duchesse
dur-e (adj)		hard
Duxelles	ct18	Duxelles
eau (f)		water
eau-de-vie (f)	tt27	eau-de-vie, a brandy
éclair (m)	tt17	éclair
écrevisse (f)		crayfish
électricité (f)		electricity
emmenthal (m)		a cheese
en		in
endive (f)		chicory
entrecôte (f)	tt10	entrecôte steak
Entre-deux-Mers		a Bordeaux wine-producing district
entrée (f)	tt1	entrée
entremettier		vegetable cook
entremets (m)	tt1	entremets, dessert
épaule (f)		shoulder
épice (f)		spice
épinards (m pl)		spinach
escalope (f)	tt11	escalope
escargot (m)		snail
espagnole (f)	tt9	espagnole, brown roux
estouffade (f)	tt18	estouffade, brown stock
estragon (m)		tarragon
éventail (m)		fan
faisan (m)		pheasant
farci-e (adj)		stuffed
faux, fausse (adj)		false
fausse tortue (f)		mock turtle
fécule (f)	tt18	fécule, starch
fenouil (m)		fennel
fermière (adj)	ct19	fermière; lit. in the style of the farmer's wife

feuille (f)		leaf
feuille de laurier (f)		bay-leaf
fève (f)		broad bean
Figeac (Château)		a St-Emilion wine
figue (f)		fig
filet (m)		fillet
filtre (m)		filter
café filtre (m)		filter coffee
fine (f)		high quality brandy
fine champagne (f)		
fines herbes (f)	tt9	fines herbes
fixe (adj)		fixed
Fixin (m)		a Côte de Nuits commune; a wine
flageolet (m)		white haricot bean, flageolet
flamande (adj)	ct4	flamande; in Flemish style
flambé (adj)	tt&ct20	flambé
flan (m)		flan; custard cream
Flazey-Echézeaux		a Côte de Nuits commune; a wine
flétan (m)		halibut
fleurie (m)		a Beaujolais wine
florentine (adj)	ct4	florentine; in the style of Florence
Florida	ct2	Florida
flûte (f)		champagne glass
foie (m)		liver
fond (m) d'artichaut		artichoke heart, base
fond (m) (de cuisine)		stock
fondant -e (adj)		melting, fondant
fondue (f)	tt14	fondue
fontainebleau (m)	tt14	fontainebleau, cheese and cream dessert
fouet (m)		whisk
fouetté (adj)		whipped
four (m)		oven
petits fours (m pl)	tt27	petits fours
Fourtet (Clos)		a St-Emilion wine
fourchette (f)		fork
frais, fraîche (adj)		cool, fresh
fraise (f)		strawberry
framboise (f)		raspberry
franc (m)		franc
français -e (adj)		French
France (f)		France
Francfort	ct11	Frankfurt
frappé (adj)		chilled, cooled
friandise (f)		delicacy, sweetmeat

fricassé (adj)	tt10	fricassé
frit -e (adj)		fried
froid -e (adj)		cold
fromage (m)		cheese
fruit (m)		fruit
fruits de mer (m pl)		sea-food
fumé (adj)		smoked
fumet (m)	tt4	fumet, essence
galantine (f)	tt13	galantine
Gamay		variety of grape
garbure (f)	tt4	garbure
garçon (de café) (m)		waiter
Gard (m)		department in the south of France
garni (adj)		garnished
Garonne (f)		river in the south-west of France
Gascogne (f)		Gascony
gâteau (m)	tt17	gâteau, cake
gaufrette (f)	tt8	gaufrette, waffle
gaz (m)		gas
gazeux -se (adj)		gassy, fizzy, sparkling
gelée (f)		jelly, jam
Gervais		make of yoghurt; cheese
Gevrey-Chambertin (m)		a Côte de Nuits commune; a wine
gewürztraminer (m)		an Alsace wine
gibier (m)		game
Gigondas (m)		a Côtes du Rhône wine
gigot (m)		leg of mutton, gigot
Gironde (f)		estuary of the Garonne
gîte à la noix (m)		silverside
glace (f)		glaze; ice cream
glacé		glazed
gnocchi (It)	tt9	gnocchi
goujon (m)	tt5	goujon, strip
goujonnette (f)		small goujon
grain (m)	ct13	grain
grand -e (adj)		large, big
Grand Marnier (m)		a liqueur
gras -se (adj)		fat, fatty
pâté de foie gras	tt3	pâté de foie gras
gratin (m) au	tt6	au gratin
gratiné (adj)		au gratin
Graves (m)		a Bordeaux wine and region
grec, grecque (adj)		Greek
à la grecque	ct2	à la grecque, in Greek style

Grenache		a variety of grape
grenouille (f)		frog
gril (m)		grill
grillade (f)		grilled food
grillé (adj)		grilled
groseille (f)		red currant
grouse (m)		grouse
gruyère (m)		a cheese
Guiraud (Château)		a Sauternes wine
hachis (m)		mince (meat)
haché (adj)		minced
hanche (f)		haunch
hareng (m)		herring
haricot (m)		green bean, runner bean
haut -e (adj)		high, tall
Haut-Bailly (Château)		a Graves wine
Haut-Brion (Château)		a Graves wine
Haut-Médoc (Le)		wine-producing region of Bordeaux
Hennessy		a brandy
Henri IV	ct11	Henri IV
Hérault (m)		a department in the south of France
herbe (f)		herb
Hermitage (m)		a Côtes du Rhône wine
Hine		a brandy
hollandaise	ct18	hollandaise; in Dutch style
homard (m)		lobster
hongroise	ct18	hongroise; in Hungarian style
hors-d'oeuvre (m)	tt1	hors-d'oeuvre
hôte (m)		host or guest
huile (f)		oil
huître (f)		oyster
ici		here
par ici		this way
île flottante (f)	tt17	île flottante; lit. floating island
impératrice	ct17	impératrice; in the style of the Empress
indienne	ct19	indienne; in Indian style
intérêt public (m)		public interest, concern
izarra jaune (f)		a liqueur
verte		
Jacques	ct15	Jacques
jambon (m)		ham

jardinière	ct7	jardinière; in gardener's style
jaune		yellow
je		I
jour (m)		day
Judic	ct19	Judic
juliénas (m)		a Beaujolais wine
julienne (f)	tt&ct4	julienne
jus (m)		juice; gravy
kirsch (m)		a liqueur
Krug		a variety of champagne
lait (m)		milk
laitance (f)		fish roe
laitue (f)		lettuce
langouste (f)		spiny lobster
langoustine (f)		small lobster, Dublin Bay prawn
langue (f)		tongue
langue de chat		a biscuit
Languedoc (m)		a region in southern France
lapin (m)		rabbit
lard (m)		bacon, bacon fat
lasagne (It)	tt9	lasagne
laurier (m)		bay-leaf
feuille de		
La Tour-Blanche		a Sauternes wine
La Tour-Figeac		a St-Emilion wine
lave-vaisselle (m)		dish-washer
le, la, les, l'		the
légume (m)		vegetable
lentilles (f) pl		lentils
liaison (f)	tt18	liaison, thickening agent
lié (adj)		thickened
lieu (m)		pollack
lièvre (m)		hare
liqueur (f)		liqueur
litre (m)		litre
Loire (f)		river Loire
lotte (f)		burbot
longe (f)		loin
louche (f)		ladle
lyonnaise (adj)	ct4	lyonnaise; in the style of Lyon (Lyons)
macaroni (It)	tt9	macaroni
macédoine (f)	tt19	mixed fruit or vegetables, macédoine

Mâcon		important town in Burgundy
Mâconnais, Côte du		wine-producing region of Burgundy
madame (f)		madam
madère (m)		madeira
madrilène	ct4	madrilène; in Madrid style
maïs (m)		sweetcorn
maison (f)	ct3	home-made, house
maître d'hôtel (m)	tt19	maître d'hôtel, head waiter
mange-tout (m)		stringless 'haricot vert'
maquereau (m)		mackerel
marc (m)	tt27	marc, eau-de-vie
maréchale (adj)	ct13	maréchale; in marshal style
Marengo	ct11	Marengo
Margaux (m)		a Bordeaux commune and wine
marié (adj)		
petite mariée	ct13	petite mariée; lit. young married woman
marinière (adj)	ct6	marinière; in marine style; mariner style
marmite (f)		stockpot
petite marmite	ct4	petite marmite
Marne (f)		river in north-east France
marque (f)		make, type
marquise (f)	ct8	marquise; Marchioness
marron (m)		chestnut
marsala (m)		marsala
Martell		a brandy
mayonnaise (f)	tt2	mayonnaise
médaillon (m)	ct11	médaillon
Médoc (le)		wine-producing region near Bordeaux
Haut-Médoc (m)		part of Médoc
Melba	ct15	Melba
melon (m)		melon
menthe (f)		mint
menu (m)		menu
mer (f)		sea
merci		thank you
merci beaucoup		thank you very much
Mercier		a variety of champagne
meringue (f)	tt17	meringue
merlan (m)		whiting
meunière	ct6	meunière; in the style of the miller's wife
Meursault (m)		a Beaune wine; the commune
Midi (m)		Midi, south of France

miel (m)		honey
mignon -ne (adj)		small, neat
milanaise (adj)	ct7	milanaise; in the style of Milan
mille		thousand
mille-feuille (m)	tt17	mille-feuille
feuilles (pl)		
mimosa	ct9	mimosa
minérale (eau) (adj)		mineral (water)
minute (f)	ct10	minute
mirabelle (f)		mirabelle plum
mirepoix (f)	tt19	mirepoix
mis		put, placed
mis en bouteille		bottled
mise en bouteille (f)		the process of bottling
mode (f)		method
à la mode de Caen	ct12	à la mode de Caen
Moët et Chandon		a champagne
moka (m)		mocha
mollet (adj)		soft
montagne (f)		mountain
Montmorency	ct16	Montmorency
Morey-St-Denis (m)		a Côte de Nuits commune and wine
morgon (m)		a Beaujolais wine
Mornay	tt&ct14	Mornay
morue (f)		cod (dried, salted)
moulin-à-vent (m)		a Beaujolais wine
moule (f)		mussel
mousse (f)	tt16	mousse
mousseline (f)		purée (of potatoes), lit. muslin
mousseux -se (adj)		sparkling
moutarde (f)		mustard
mouton (m)		sheep, mutton
mûre (f)		blackberry
muscat d'Alsace (m)		an Alsace wine
muscade (f)		nutmeg
muscadet (m)		a Loire valley wine
navarin (m)	tt11	navarin, lamb stew
navet (m)		turnip
nature	ct8	natural, plain
neige, à la (f)	ct8	(snow) à la neige
Nevers		town in central France
niçoise (adj)	ct2	niçoise; in the style of Nice
noir -e (adj)		black
noisette (f)		hazelnut; 'noisette' cut of lamb
noix (f)		walnut

(gîte) à la noix		silverside
noix muscade		nutmeg
non		no
normande (adj)	ct19	normande; in the style of Normandy
Normandie (la)		Normandy, region in northern France
norvégienne (adj)	ct17	norvégienne; in Norwegian style
nouveau, nouvelle (adj)		new
nouille (f) (usually in pl)		noodle
Nuits, Côte de		wine-producing region in Burgundy
Nuits-St-Georges		town in the Côte de Nuits; the wine of that commune
ocuf (m)		egg
oie (f)		goose
oignon (m)		onion
olive (f)		olive
omelette (f)		omelette
orange (f)		orange
ordinaire (adj)		ordinary
oui		yes
ouvre-boîte (m)		tin-opener
paille (f)		straw
pain (m)		bread
palmier (m)		palm-leaf biscuit
pamplemousse (m)		grapefruit
panaché (adj)		mixed
panais (m)		parsnip
pané (adj)	tt20	pané; breadcrumbed
paprika (m)		paprika
par		by, through
par ici		this way
parfumé (adj)		flavoured
Parmentier	ct4	Parmentier
parmesan (m)		a cheese
partie, chef de (f)		head of section (in the kitchen)
passoire (f)		strainer
pâte (f) (les pâtes)		pasta
pâté (m)	tt3	pâté
pâté de foie		liver pâté
pâtisserie (f)	tt	pâtisserie, pastries, cakes
pâtissier, chef		head pastry cook
Pauillac (m)		a Médoc commune and a wine
paupiette (f)	tt4	paupiette

pays (m)		country, district
pêche (f)		peach
perdreau (m)		partridge (young)
perdrix (m)		partridge
Périgueux	ct19	Périgueux
Pernand-Vergelesses (m)		a Beaune commune and wine
Perrier (m)		a bottled water
persil (m)		parsley
persillé (adj)		sprinkled with parsley
petit -e (adj)		small
Petit-Village (Château)		a Pomerol wine
pétillant -e (adj)		sparkling
Petrus (Château)		a Pomerol wine
peu		few, little
un peu		a few, a little
pied (m)		foot
pilaf	ct9	pilaf
piment (m)		pimento
pintade (f)		guinea-fowl
pintadeau (m)		young guinea-fowl
pinot noir		a variety of grape
pinot blanc		a variety of grape
piquante	ct11	piquante; lit. prickly, stinging
pithiviers (m)	tt17	Pithiviers cake
plaît		
s'il vous plaît		please
plat (m)		plate, dish
sur le plat		fried (egg)
plat du jour		dish of the day
plateau (m)		large dish
plie (f)		plaice
plus		more
en plus		in addition
plutôt		rather
poché		poached
poêle (f)		frying-pan
poêlé (adj)		shallow fried
point		
à point		medium rare (steak)
pointe (f)		tip
poire (f)		pear
poireau (m)		leek
pois (m)		pea
poisson (m)		fish
poitrine (f)		breast
poivre (f)		pepper
poivron (m)		a pepper

Pol Roger		a champagne
Pomerol (m)		a wine-producing district near Bordeaux
Pommard (m)		a Beaune commune and a wine
pomme (f)		apple
pomme de terre (f)		potato
Pommery et Greno		a champagne
Pont-Neuf	ct8	Pont-Neuf; lit. new bridge
pont-l'évêque (m)		a cheese
porc (m)		pork
porto (m)		port
port salut (m)		a cheese
portugaise	ct4	portugaise; in Portuguese style
potage (m)		soup
pot-au-feu (m)	tt10	pot-au-feu; lit. pot-on-the-fire
poularde (f)		pullet
poule (f) poulet (m)		chicken
pouilly fumé (m)		a Loire Valley wine
pouilly-fuissé (m)		a Mâcon wine
pourriture noble (f)		'noble rot'
poussin (m)		pullet
praliné (adj)	tt16	praliné
premier -ère (adj)		first
prendrai		
je prendrai		I'll have, I'll take
prenez-vous?		will you have? will you take?
pré-salé (m)	ct19	pré-salé; lit. salt meadow
primeurs (m pl) les		early vegetables
principal -e (adj)		principal, main
printanier -ère	ct19	printanier -ère; spring-like
printemps (m)		spring
prix (m)		price
profiterole (f)	tt17	profiterole
propriété (f)		property, estate
provençale	ct19	provençale; in the style of Provence
Provence la		region in the Midi
Côtes de Provence		wine district in the Midi
prune (f)		plum
pruneau (m)		prune
purée (f)	tt4	purée
qualité (f)		quality
quart (m)		quarter
quatrième		fourth
que?		what?
quenelle (f)	tt6	quenelle

qu'est-ce que (c'est?)		what?, what is it?
queue (f)		tail
quiche lorraine (f)	tt14	quiche lorraine
râble (m)		saddle of hare
radis (m)		radish
rafraîchi -e (adj)		chilled
ragoût (m)		stew
raie (f)		skate
raifort (m)		horse-radish
raisin (m)		grapes
râpe (f)		grater
râpé (adj)		grated
ratatouille (f)	tt7	ratatouille
recommandé (adj)		recommended
Réforme	ct11	Réforme
réfrigérateur (m)		refrigerator
Reims		Rheims
reine (f)		queen
bouchée à la reine	tt11	cf 'bouchée' — lit. a mouthful
relevé (m)	tt1	relevé
rémoulade (f)	tt2	rémoulade
Rémy Martin		a brandy
renversé (adj)		
crème renversée		caramel custard
Rhône le		French river
Côtes du Rhône		wine-producing region south of Lyon
rhum (m)		rum
riche (adj)		rich; sweet (of champagne)
richebourg (m)		a Côte de Nuits wine
riesling (m)		an Alsace wine
rillettes (f pl)	tt7	rillettes
ris (m)		sweetbread
risotto (m)	tt9	risotto
riz (m)		rice
robe (f) de chambre } robe des champs }		'in the jacket' potatoes
Robert	ct18	Robert
rognon (m)		kidney
romain -e (adj)	tt9	romaine; in Roman style
romarin (m)		rosemary
roquefort (m)		a blue cheese
rosé (adj)		pink
rosé (m)		rosé (wine)
rosé d'Anjou (m)		a Loire Valley wine
Rossini	ct11	Rossini

rôti (adj)		roast
rôtisseur, chef (m)		chef de partie (for roasting)
rouennaise (adj)	ct13	rouennaise; in the style of Rouen
rouge (adj)		red
rouge (m)		red wine
rouleau (m)		rolling-pin
royale (f)	tt4	royale
Ruinart		a champagne
russe (adj)		Russian
sabayon (m)	tt17	sabayon
safran (m)		saffron
saignant (adj)		very rare (steak)
St-Amour (m)		a Beaujolais wine
St-Emilion (m)		a region of Bordeaux; a wine
St-Estèphe (m)		a commune of the Médoc; a wine
St-Germain	ct4	St-Germain
St-Julien (m)		a Bordeaux wine (Médoc)
St-Nazaire		a town at the mouth of the Loire
st-paulin (m)		a cheese
saison (f)		season
salade (f)		salad
salami (m)	tt3	salami
salmis (m)	tt12	salmis, stew of feathered game
sancerre (m)		a Loire Valley wine
Saône, la		river in central France
sardine (f)		sardine
sauce (f)		sauce, gravy
saucier (chef)		chef de partie (for sauces)
saucisse (f)		sausage
saucisson (m)		preserved sausage (for slicing)
sauge (f)		sage
saumon (m)		salmon
saumur (m)		wine of the Loire Valley
sauté (adj)	tt8	sauté
sauteuse (f)		sauté pan
Sauternes (m)		wine-producing region near Bordeaux; a Bordeaux wine
savarin (m)	tt17	savarin
Savigny-les-Beaunes (m)		a Beaune commune; a wine
scampi (m) (It)		scampi
sec, sèche (adj)		dry
seigle (m)		rye
sel (m)		salt
selle (f)		saddle
serveur -se (m of f)		waiter, waitress

service (m)		service
sirop (m)		syrup
sole (f)		sole
sommelier (m)		wine-waiter
sorbet (m)	tt16	sorbet
Soubise	ct18	Soubise
soucoupe (f)		saucer
soufflé (m)	tt17	soufflé
soupe (f)	tt4	soupe, soup
source (f)		spring
eau-de-source		spring water (bottled)
sous-chef (m)		deputy chef of cuisine
spaghetti (m) (It)		spaghetti
steak (m) (Eng)		steak
Stroganoff	ct12	Stroganoff
sucre (m)		sugar
sucré (adj)		sweetened, sugared
suisse (adj)		Swiss
petit suisse (m)		a cheese
suivre		
à suivre		to follow
supérieur -e (adj)		superior
suprême (m) and (adj)	tt13	suprême
surprise (f)	tt17	surprise
sus		
en sus		in addition, not included
Suzette	ct17	Suzette
sylvaner (m)		a wine of Alsace
table (f)		table
table d'hôte	tt1	table d'hôte
Taittinger		a champagne
tamis (m)		strainer, tamis cloth
tartare (adj)	ct18	tartar
tasse (f)		cup, bowl
tavel (m)		a wine from the Côtes du Rhône
taxe (f)		tax
terrine (f)	tt3	terrine; an earthenware dish
thé (m)		tea
thon (m)		tunny, tuna
thym (m)		thyme
Tia Maria		a liqueur
tilleul (m)		lime, an infusion
tire-bouchon (m)		cork-screw
tisane (f)	tt21	tisane, infusion
tokay d'Alsace (m)		an Alsace wine
tomate (f)		tomato

tomme de Savoie (f)		a cheese
torchon (m)		cloth
tortue (f)		turtle
toulousain -e (adj)	ct7	toulousaine; from Toulouse
Tours		town in France
tournedos (m)	tt10	tournedos steak
tournesol (m)		sunflower
tout		all, everything
tout compris		inclusive
traminer (m)		an Alsace wine
triple sec (m)		a liqueur
troisième (adj)		third
tronçon (m)		cutlet (of fish)
truffe (f)		truffle
truffé (adj)		with truffles
truite (f)		trout
tuile (f)		tile
Turbigo	ct12	Turbigo
turbot (m)		turbot
tutti frutti (It)	tt15	tutti frutti; lit. all fruit
un, une		a, an
vacherin (m)	tt15	vacherin
Val de Loire (m)		Loire Valley; wine-producing district
Valence		town in the south of France
vanille (f)		vanilla
vapeur (f)		steam
varié (adj)		varied
Vaucrains les		a Nuits-St-Georges 'village'; a wine
vaudésir (m)		a chablis
veau (m)		veal
velouté (m)	tt4	velouté
venaison (f)		large game
vermicelli (It)		a pasta
Véronique	ct6	Véronique
verre (m)		glass
vert -e (adj)		green
vert-pré	ct11	vert-pré (green meadow)
verveine (f)		verbena, an infusion
verveine du Velay (f)		a liqueur
Veuve Clicquot		a champagne
viande (f)		meat
Vichy	ct7	Vichy
vichyssoise (adj)	tt4	vichyssoise

Vieille Cure (f)		a liqueur
Vienne		town in southern France
viennoise (adj)	ct11	viennoise; lit. from Vienna
village (m)		village
vin (m)		wine
vinaigre (m)		vinegar
vinaigrette (f)	tt2	vinaigrette
Vire		a town in France
Vittel (m)		a spring water (bottled)
Vitteloise		a spring water (bottled)
voici		here is, here are
volaille (f)		poultry
vol-au-vent (m)	tt13	vol-au-vent
Volnay (m)		a Beaune commune; a wine
Volvic (m)		a spring water (bottled)
Vosges les		mountains in eastern France
Vosne-Romanée (m)		a Côte de Nuits commune; a wine
voudrais		
je voudrais		I would like
Vougeot (m)		a Côte de Nuits commune; a wine
voulez		
voulez-vous?		would you like?
vous		you
vouvray (m)		a Loire Valley wine
voyons		let's see
Washington	ct7	Washington
yaourt (m)		yoghurt
Yquem, Château d'		a Sauternes wine

144

Supplementary notes